WAY BACK THEN

Edited by

Andrew Head

First published in Great Britain in 1999 by
POETRY NOW
1-2 Wainman Road, Woodston,
Peterborough, PE2 7BU
Telephone (01733) 230746
Fax (01733) 230751

All Rights Reserved

Copyright Contributors 1999

HB ISBN 0 75430 580 5
SB ISBN 0 75430 581 3

FOREWORD

Although we are a nation of poetry writers we are accused of not reading poetry and not buying poetry books: after many years of listening to the incessant gripes of poetry publishers, I can only assume that the books they publish, in general, are books that most people do not want to read.
Poetry should not be obscure, introverted, and as cryptic as a crossword puzzle: it is the poet's duty to reach out and embrace the world.
The world owes the poet nothing and we should not be expected to dig and delve into a rambling discourse searching for some inner meaning.
The reason we write poetry (and almost all of us do) is because we want to communicate: an ideal; an idea; or a specific feeling.
Poetry is as essential in communication, as a letter; a radio; a telephone, and the main criteria for selecting the poems in this anthology is very simple: they communicate.

CONTENTS

The Way We Were	Ivy Cawood	1
Tell Us Again	June Marshall	2
Reflections On A Wall	Dorothy Campbell	3
The Past And The Present	Robert Doherty	4
Advancement	David Rhine	5
The 'Saving Kitchen Waste' Campaign 1941	Amy I Cotter	6
The Good Old Days	Elwynne	7
The Good Old Days	Jenny Hornsey	8
Nostalgia Isn't What It Used To Be	Andrew Fisher	9
The Good Old Days	Elaine Beresford	10
Those Were The Days	Lyrica Dearne	11
Schooldays In Yorkshire	Janet Hewitt	12
Village Milkmaid	Margaret E Dowson	13
The Way We Were!	Eva Rose	14
Stately Reserve	Helga Hopkinson	16
Vanishing Cream	Heather Bruyére Watt	18
Aubrey Beardsly Where Are You?	Michael Soper	19
The Warehouses	Ann Ridley	20
Tenement Folk	Paddy Jupp	22
Nostalgia	Margaret Ballard	23
World War II 1939-1945	D Naylor	24
The Way We Were	Hugh Sturrock	25
Back In The 1890's	Barbara Fosh	26
Saturday Matinee	Raymond Winston Aspden	27
Basic Bliss	A F Allen	28
Untitled	Daisy Arkwright	29
Times Past	Elizabeth Walker	30
Cheerful Days!	Hilary Jill Robson	32
'In The Good Old, Bad Old Days . . .'	Denis Martindale	33
All Our Yesterdays	F Gerrard	34
Today Or Yesterday - Which Is Really Advanced?	Helen Georgeou	35

1940's Grammar School	Joan Knight	36
Play Rock 'N' Roll For Me	Roger J Gould	37
Holding My Breath	Susan Roberts	38
The Way We Were In Wartime	Ellen W Worthington	40
The Hungry Thirties	Joan G Railiffe	41
Remember?	Joan Hands	42
Only The Old . . .	Joan Letts	43
The Good Old Days	Hubert Hayes	44
Bare Facts	Mary Skelton	45
Grandma's Photo Album	N M Beddoes	46
'New' For 'Old'	Cindy White	47
Sisters Going To The Petty	Jean Sweeney	48
I Remember Stanley	R Chapman	49
The Way We Were	Alice M Archer	50
The Way We Were	Jean Rendell	51
Reflections	Margaret Knox Stubbs	52
The Good Old Days	Barbara Ann Barker	53
Way Back Then	B C Watts	54
I Remember	Paul Gold	56
Suburban Almanac Of The Thirties	Gillian C Fisher	57
The Halfpenny Tram	Chris Senior	58
The Good Old Days	G Silver	59
My Family	Elizabeth Parish	60
Nostalgia	Patricia Farley	61
The Way We Were	Marguerite Brassington-Griffiths	62
Untitled	Raymond John Mandeville	63
The Lane	Gwenneth Woodall	64
Grandma's Memories	Tracy Howie	65
Song Of The Shirt	Wyn Cornish	66
The Way We Were	Joan Patrickson	68
Happy Days	P M Wardle	69
The Good Old Days	John Hickman	70
The Evacuees	Ann May Wallace	71
Tea Rations	Pam Quigley	72
When Gran Was Young	Jean Roslyn Carr	73
Reminiscence	T G Bloodworth	74

Title	Author	Page
Passing Days	Joan Hawkes	75
Words On War	David A Garside	76
The Stuff Of Dreams	Una Ellis	77
The Good Old Days	Yvonne King	78
Old Hippies Never Die . . .	Russell Adams	79
A Farm Called Hope	Rebecca Pine	80
The Way We Were	I Price	81
Students' Hops	Rhoda D Strath	82
The Way We Were	Mary McPhee	83
Memories Of Yesteryear	Iris Taylor	84
Christmas Past	R M Jeff	85
Over Fifty Years Ago	K Coleman	86
Childhood Revisited	J R Springthorpe	87
The Horse	B Salter	88
Thirties' Teenager	Joan R Gilmour	89
On Sundays	Bea Budd	90
As We Were	Enid Gill	91
Those Days	Caz Fisher	92
Above All Else	Jessie Morton	93
A Word To The Wise	Kim Montia	94
Bristol Blitz 1940	Margaret Carl Hibbs	95
Bygone Days	Frieda Cox	96
Yo-Yo Memories	B G Clarke	97
Memories	D A Broad	98
The Corn Stooks	Valerie Ovais	99
A Forties' Child	Catherine Reay	100
Times Past	June Witt	101
Lazy Days	Geraldine Bruce	102
Lancashire Wakes	F B Broomfield	103
Through The Eyes Of A Child	David Ford	104
Mill Town (1940)	John Widdows	105
Newspapers And Troops Only . . .	Peter Hicks	106
The Way We Were	Jean Calver	107
Touch The Past	Claire-Lyse Sylvester	108
Where?	E B Holcombe	109
I Remember	M Muirhead	110
Saturday Morning	John Aldred	111

Whispering Memories	Collin West	112
Oranges	B Neave	113
Home	Barbara King	114
Policemen Smiled	Fiona Bower	115
The Picture Palaces	William W M Campbell	116
Those Were The Days	Anne Brown	118
The Way We Were	Michael Carter	119
War	Margaret Roe	120
Christmas Long Ago	Eileen Burton	121
The Way We Were	Geoff Rivers	122
One Day At A Time	Claire Marie O'Connor	124

The Way We Were

The cycle of time moves far, far away
From the pleasures we knew of yesterday,
With simple joys and leisurely pace,
Compared with today's mad, hectic race.

Serenity, calm, and children's joys
On opening a stocking (with not many toys)
Some wondered how Santa had managed his sack
Climbing the chimney with sack on his back?

Ah, now it's computers and no expense spared,
Today's children don't know how yesterday's fared!
Oh no! Now a pillowcase lies there instead.

Yes, times gone by were better by far,
No road jams, motorways, or killings by car.
But each age has its day, move on! So they say,
Just keep going on; and hold memories at bay.

So I'll go with the rest and stampede; do my best
To keep pace with the speed of today,
But still think of the calm of yesteryear's balm,
And my memories are flowers in May.

Ivy Cawood

TELL US AGAIN

Grandma please tell us just once more
Stories about what life was like
When families didn't own a car
And your dearest wish was to have a bike.
We love to hear how you used to go
Off to the woods with your sandwich pack
Along with your pals out of grown-ups' way.
How they grumbled if you were early back.
And what about those newspaper squares
You had to use in the outside loo
And that chamber pot beneath the bed.
Are you kidding or was that really true?
Wind-up gramophones. Coal fires to make.
How did you manage? It sounds like hell.
No television. Gas mantles for light.
You wouldn't lie, we know you too well.
Did you never want to go abroad?
Well where *did* you go for your holiday?
To the nearest seaside. What if it rained?
So you *did* have cinemas in your day.
It was sad that your best friend's accident
Meant she would never walk again.
Could nothing be done for the poor young girl?
Such a miserable life with all that pain.
But that was sixty-five years ago,
Today's surgery might have done the trick.
Well look at the way *you* move around
Since you got your artificial hip.

June Marshall

Reflections On A Wall

I sit on a wall and think of the days
When the roads were dirty and full of haze.
And all of the paths were covered in dust
And men rode on horseback, because they must.
There was no other way to go but walk
And people did nothing much else but talk -
Unless they were working hard at their trades
Weaving cloth and baskets, or using spades
To dig up the soil and grow all their crops
And brew their own wine, conserving the drops.
They cut down the trees for firewood sticks
And used clay and sand to make their own bricks.

There wasn't much time for playing the fool
And not all the children were sent to school.

Now, as I look at the sky and the trees
And feel around me a welcoming breeze,
The sound of the traffic, thundering by,
Disturbs conversation and makes me sigh
For the days that are past, when life was slow
And everybody had somewhere to go.

When rich people plotted and poor ones died
Because there was simply nowhere to hide.
From cradle to grave a man's course was planned.
He couldn't escape from his master's hand.
There was no reprieve to brighten his life -
He died as he'd lived - and so did his wife.

There still isn't time for playing the fool,
But most of the children are sent to school.

Dorothy Campbell

The Past And The Present

I can remember the good old days
When life was more enjoyable in many ways
More children cycled or walked to school
Many spent some time at a swimming pool
Adults also took more exercise
The way people lived could be classed as wise
There were less vehicles on the roads unlike today
So the air was healthier in every way.

A person used to be able to go out and do a chore
Without having to worry about locking or closing the door
One could go out at any time of night or day
With no fear of danger in any way
Sadly one has to be careful nowadays
And watch other people's actions in all ways
In the good old days people had more trust in each other
Just like the trust a child has in its mother

In the good old days more neighbours got together
And on many a subject they had a good blether
This would have got many a problem off their chest
At night they were able to get a good rest
Many could not afford to buy a lot
But they were happy with what they had got
People helped others in every way
And for this they did not demand a reward or any pay

Robert Doherty

ADVANCEMENT

Twenty people have waited an hour
For an overdue bus that has yet to come.
Twenty people would have been home
If we still rode horses instead of machines.

David Rhine

THE 'SAVING KITCHEN WASTE' CAMPAIGN 1941
(The Pig's Bin)

In 1941 they planned a use for our waste food -
To save it up for little pigs and make them fat and good.
So heavy bins, like dustbins, every street would host,
And solidly they stood their ground beneath the street's lamp post.

They would receive our peelings from potatoes and from fruit,
And there we put our old pea pods and bits of old beetroot.
What did we do with all the scraps left over from the roast?
We dropped them in the pigs' bin down by our lamp post!

A porker's smiling picture winked at us from the bin,
As if to say, 'Bring all your waste, roll up and throw it in,
Come with your greens and give us beans, and things we like the most.
Just drop 'em in the pigs' bin down by this lamp post.

Every little fattens us, so give us all your pips.
Give us all your leavings from your bag of fish and chips.
Even keep the tiny crumbs from off your morning toast,
And put 'em in the pigs' bin down by this lamp post.

So when we went out shopping to buy a piece of meat,
The pork chops in the butcher's shop all looked a perfect treat!
When they were cooked and sizzling hot, about our pork we'd boast,
'Cos we'd saved waste food for pigs' bins down by each lamp post.

Amy I Cotter

The Good Old Days

Oh I remember yesteryears
Of childhood life in village dear.
Where everybody was a friend.
In troubled times - neighbours would lend
A helping hand to those in need.

Windows and back doors opened wide.
Friendly neighbours popped inside,
Bringing us new or small wee gift.
Offering sympathy or a lift
To butcher's shop or post office.

Delivery man brought groceries round,
Left them on table if he found
No one indoors . . . go on his way;
For he would know that Mum would pay
Him the next morning without fail.

On Tuesdays came the muffin man.
Hearing his call . . . we children ran
From kitchen to the garden gate.
Eager, expectant we would wait,
Knowing we'd muffins for our tea.

The toffee apple man would come
On Thursday afternoons and Mum
Would make us sit on garden seat
And not run round . . . grinning we'd eat
Caramel-coated red apples.

On Saturdays came the ice cream man.
He rode a bike . . . not ice cream van.
He would ride past us . . . just for fun.
His slogan read 'Stop me - buy one' -
We'd chase him clutching our pennies.

Elwynne

THE GOOD OLD DAYS

Ploughs were horse-drawn in those times
Our gentle giants were Beauty and Dimes
Plodding the furrow on a spring day
Harness and tackle in polished array

Pulling the carts of potatoes for store
Standing while baskets were emptied - and more
were picked and loaded atop
Homeward bound at the completion of crop

Dad would set me aside Beauty's back
As we moved and collected each haystack
Just the hum of bees and soft summertime
Idyllic days if the weather was fine

Slow and reliable it has to be said
But stables need tending and mouths to be fed
No mechanisation - just the horses' neigh
In the good old days - that was the way.

Jenny Hornsey

NOSTALGIA ISN'T WHAT IT USED TO BE

Old things seem to keep returning
As everyone has a yearning
For an era they liked -
Remembered BMX and Chopper bikes?
Dismissed as just another phase
But still valuable these days
As men remember being boys;
And the same applies to toys
The yo-yo keeps coming back
As does the Scalectrix track
Yet a modern fad like Pogs
Soon disappears and 'pops its clogs'.
In fashion there is nothing new
The mini-skirt or platform shoe,
Even flares that once went out of style
Suddenly became hip again for a while
Now it's the eighties revived
With New Romantics still alive
I must admit I hated that sound
And still do second time around!

Andrew Fisher

THE GOOD OLD DAYS

Is it really thirty years since we walked to school?
Rough tumbling, scuffing polished shoes, acting the fool.
No cars clogged the streets, in those far-off carefree days,
Parents didn't need to watch their child with anxious gaze.
A whip and top brought great delight, glass marbles were a treasure,
Viewing television didn't fill the hours of leisure,
We were Robin Hood or Biggles hiding notes in secret places,
Members of a gang solving strange, mysterious cases.
Breathless we read stories, which fired imagination,
The woods and fields, birds, trees and flowers all held our fascination.
Life was simpler then, people didn't spend, spend, spend,
All we needed was a happy home and company of a friend.

Elaine Beresford

THOSE WERE THE DAYS

Every Monday morning it became habitual
To get up very early and begin the washday ritual.
First, you fill the copper with what water it can hold,
Then light the fire beneath, and hope that it will hold,
Get the clothes together, and sort them into piles,
Put the tubs and rubbing board on the kitchen tiles.
Fix the lines up in the garden, get the bag of pegs,
And don't forget you're going to need the good old 'peggy-legs'.
Now the work of washing really can begin,
Until the clothes are looking as clean as a new pin.
Washing, rinsing, starching, and hanging on the line,
Hoping that the weather is going to keep fine.
When they're dry, we bring them in, hoping they're not tangled.
Everything is folded, then they're duly mangled
Ready for the flat iron, heated on the stove,
Pressed, and hung to air upon the line above.
Those days have gone, thank goodness, and will no more be seen
For we've gone automatic, with our brand new machine.

Lyrica Dearne

SCHOOLDAYS IN YORKSHIRE
(In the 1950s)

People talk fondly about 'The Good Old Days',
With no luxuries, we recognise now, at all.
Only 'the better off' enjoyed proper holidays;
Torn newspaper on a nail of the lavvy wall.

Christmas oranges, wrapped in purple tissue,
So exciting, the tissue as much as the fruit,
Shared out - for the lavvy an unusual queue;
Though washday stains for our mam didn't suit.

Monday was washday in Yorkshire, every week,
When our mams toiled non-stop through the day.
Tea was always cold meat and bubble 'n' squeak:
We couldn't see the fires, clothes in the way.

Sunday night was bath night, traditionally.
We had to go to bed with our hair still wet,
After it was treated with the dreaded DDT;
The obnoxious smell of it I will never forget.

Jack Frost made patterns *inside* our windows
And it was hard to get to sleep in our beds.
Especially I remember my freezing cold toes;
We wrapped knitted scarves round our heads.

Our feet were numb inside our winter wellies.
They got hot-aches, if thawed out too fast.
But, we always had warm food in our bellies;
Mam's thick vegetable broth was made to last.

Us kids played rounders, the posts were gates,
Picnicked with bottles of water, bread and jam.
We wandered for miles, safely, with our mates;
Only at Christmas could our mam buy best ham.

Janet Hewitt

Village Milkmaid

Warm, creamy milk in shining pails
Fresh and new as new.
Measuring out into sparkling white cans,
. . . The farmstead is still bathed in dew.
Cans hang on fingers - stepping round village,
Magical gleam as sun slowly awakes.
Incredible cobwebs shining on hedgerows
Must linger a moment to gaze!
Waiting on doorsteps - warm smile of welcome.
Fingers feel numb as the milk is outpoured
Households awaken to work and to greeting
As the village delivery is over once more.

Margaret E Dowson

THE WAY WE WERE!

Yesterday, has been and gone forever!
Only stories are left, if we can remember.
Events that happened decades ago,
Generations before us, Granny told us so.

Then, a woman's place was at home,
Facing the household chores, all alone.
Raising the family, cooking, baking,
Bottling fruit and jam making!

Mind-boggling, to think the life they had!
Without electricity or gas at hand.
Having to chop wood to light the fire,
For warmth, cooking and to brew tea,
That was 'The way of Life', last century.

Carrying water from the well,
Struggling with a big wooden pail!
Rising at dawn to knead the dough
For bread and cakes to bake!
Forgetting tiredness and backache.

No need for a key to lock the door,
Go to the market shopping, worry no more.
If short of cash to pay at the till,
There always was that 'Good will'.
(Has become 'credit' today, I dare say).

Modern farming, was a horse and cart!
Farmers plough the fields and worked hard.
They did not know about their 'quota',
Nor how to leave land aside 'en rota'.

These yesterdays, told like a fairy tale,
They did not know any different then!
Perhaps those laurels would now be stale,
There is no going back to revive them!

Eva Rose

STATELY RESERVE

No scent
No speck of dust
No dent.

A Chinese vase
Glazed
To last.

Drapes neatly hung
Hunting scenes
No sun.

A green velvet sofa
No bare patches
No sign of life so far.

No toys
No cradle
No noise.

A writing desk
No pen or paper
No quest.

Books untouched
Behind glass
Colours matched.

A painting on the wall
Gold-framed
And tall.

A pretty lady looks forlorn
A gentleman plays with his dog
And in the background brews a storm.

Candles without a flame
Cold to the touch
No-one to blame

Helga Hopkinson

VANISHING CREAM

Once I had a pretty face
But then disgrace
Crept up apace
And I was exposed.

Wrinkles, pimples,
No more dimples,
Crows' feet prime examples
Of a reprobate's life.

Not twenty any more
More like an old whore,
So much! Now no more!
For a lady-killer like you.

I worry and care
About the cracks I see there
But with creams I repair
And pretend they're not there

As I banish and vanish from me
Those lifelines I see,
Disappearing also, I fear,
Is the you who ruined me.

Heather Bruyère Watt

AUBREY BEARDSLY
WHERE ARE YOU?

Denzil went out and was dreadfully overpowered
By the overpowering scent of the buddleia
He was dragged back, he had a temperature
We gave him sal volatile and Earl Grey tea
And told him in very few uncertain terms to stay alive
He went out of course flagrantly, voluptuously
Into the flagrant voluptuous rhododendrons
Which by this time were very strong
And got hitched to a Boots' girl in perfume
If I had only given him his asthma sniffer, and his ioniser
Then he might have been alright, neutralised with the menthol
Abundantly produced by the careless mountain streams
He should have been protected.

Michael Soper

THE WAREHOUSES

Strong voices in local dialect
Chidingly encourage youngsters
Who bend industriously
To learn their trade.

Limbs stretch at noon,
Tools briefly rest.
White sliced or stottie tastes of
Oil and tar, whatever the filling.

Tall chimneys belch waste skywards.
The men work on unheeding;
No Green Party campaigners
For their lungs or widows.

The warehouses overlook
The wide and murky Tyne
A reason for their being,
Transporter of their skills.

Within three decades,
The march of progress forces
Empty darkened shells to gaze
Upon the lonely river.

Pigeons cling to forlorn shutters,
Rusting trucks and peeling paintwork,
And the silence is unbearable,
Choking the little tributary.

No more the brazen horn
Calls the men to burst free
In a cheerful pile, on foot and bikes,
And home for tea.

Oh, young men of this 'Great Britain'!
Lost, bewildered and bereft of skills;
Now pick a number, as from the bacon queue,
And sign away another fortnight.

And as the weeks sludge into months,
The young men sink deeper into soft settees,
Wrapped in disillusion, and wearing
A shoulder chip.

Their fathers now look amazed upon the daughters
Who, brief-cased, and power-dressed,
Manage, in executive pot-planted warehouses,
Beside the gleaming river.

Ann Ridley

TENEMENT FOLK

The good old days? Now let me think -
All those poor wives tied to the sink.
Their husbands out of work, no dosh -
The good old days? A load of tosh!

Men down the boozer every night
Leaving families in a plight.
No food 'cause all the money's gawn
So send the kids down to the pawn.

No shoes on feet, old rags to wear,
Lice running wild in raggy hair.
Outside loos, newspaper sheets,
Urchins playing in trash-filled streets.

No NHS to treat the ill -
No money? Then no magic pill.
Oh life was short, full of despair
For those in tenements everywhere.

The good old days? A load of rot.
No dole, so nothing's what you got
And in the end could bear no more -
Just one more body rotting on the floor.

Paddy Jupp

Nostalgia

Mum raked out the ashes
In the cold grey dawn,
With crumpled paper, kindling wood,
So the fire was born.

Cold as ice the bedroom,
Jack Frost was here again,
Etching magic pictures
On the windowpane.

At the shout of, 'Milk-O!'
The clop of horses' feet,
With her jug she hurried
Out into the street.

Each Monday, at the copper,
She worked in clouds of steam
Then pegged the clothes upon the line,
Good drying winds her dream.

She bottled fruit in kilner jars,
Cut apple rings to dry,
Set yeasty dough to prove and rise,
Baked many a tasty pie.

When teatime came, upon the hob
The old black kettle purred,
The gaslight shed a gentle glow,
The kitten hardly stirred.

Our mother worked so hard and long,
I can't imagine how
She coped, but cope she did.
Yet is it better now?

Margaret Ballard

WORLD WAR II 1939-1945

I worked on the Lancaster bomber
In World War Number Two.
It was an honour and a privilege
To serve our lads in blue.

It was a time of great anxiety,
With our loved ones absent elsewhere
Fighting in some distant land
On the sea and in the air.

We didn't know what they went through,
We could only comprehend,
As we worked and prayed for victory
And hoped the war would end.

It was a dreadful war I would like to forget,
But I remember it with pride.
We could have lost our freedom,
But we soldiered side by side.

When victory came it was at a price
Of lost loved ones we can't forget.
They paid the ultimate sacrifice,
We thank them, with deepest regret.

D Naylor

THE WAY WE WERE

When television was in black and white
And Doctor Who gave us a fright.
Only having two channels to view
But if you were rich you had BBC2.
Now you can choose from 200 or more
With pay per view also in store.

When Alan Freeman was on Pick of the Pops
And a 45 record cost 6 bob in the shops,
On the wireless there were three programmes we heard
The Light, the Home and also the Third.
We had gramophones with three different speeds,
Now there's cassettes and mini CDs.

We had phones with dials and even a bell,
With no ansafones or things like voice mail.
Our phone boxes were once a majestic red,
Now they're yellow and even black instead.
There were real humans at the end of the line,
Not a dull, cold computerised whine.

Life seemed much slower, at an easier pace,
Unlike today where each day is a race.
When Sunday was Holy and churches were full,
A day of rest and a chance to refuel.
Life now I fear has lost all its soul,
Where money and power seem the only goal.

Hugh Sturrock

BACK IN THE 1890'S

It is not so long ago
Comparatively speaking
That things were very different
When we went pleasure-seeking.

To go aboard a liner
And take to the open sea
Would have been a great adventure
For the likes of you and me.

A lady would waft up the gangway
Clutching the arm of her beau
Elegantly dressed with a nipped-in waist
A big hat and a bustle below.

Moustached gentlemen were formally dressed,
Children in sailor suits too,
All welcomed as they climbed on board
By the Captain and his crew.

Sturdy trunks were piled on the decks
Wooden benches and the odd wicker chair,
As the funnel gave a toot toot
Excitement was in the air.

There were bunk beds in boarded cabins
With brass rails so you didn't fall out
And numbers became less in the dining room
As the ship started rolling about.

To watch obstacle races and jumping
Through barrels by the crew
Or to sit in the music or smoking room
Was something else that you could do.

Then 'Land Ahoy' arriving safe and sound
It was heaven to put your feet on the ground!

Barbara Fosh

SATURDAY MATINEE

Saturday afternoon off to the flicks
For tuppence whisked to a magical world,
Shorts, serial, adventure usual mix
As lights dimmed images on screen unfurled.

Comics of that era starred in the shorts
W C Fields, Harold Lloyd, Keaton lots more,
First film often a comedy of sorts
Laugh at Stan and Ollie, till ribs were sore.

Shirley Temple, tiny talented tot
Cartoons, with Mickey Mouse and dog Pluto,
Our Gang's Alfalfa as a freckled clot
Popeye eats spinach then flattens Bluto.

Weekly serial, hero in distress
Cliff-hanging, or inches off a saw blade,
Next episode he'd get out of the mess
Whatever threat, certain death he'd evade.

Main film starred Hollywood men of action
Johnny Weismüller wrestling jungles big cat,
Screen tough guys became major attraction
Cagney fists flying mutters 'You dirty rat.'

Errol Flynn's buccaneering 'Captain Blood'
Or as 'Robin Hood' putting wrongs to rights,
With merry band in forest of Sherwood
Outwitting the sheriff clad in green tights.

When lights came on matinee at an end
Kids reacted the parts they had just seen,
Imitating heroes, homeward would wend
In bygone golden age of silver screen.

Raymond Winston Aspden

BASIC BLISS

We lived in tiny terraced houses,
Our parents weren't partners only spouses;
The rent man called once a week
For his nine and six, which wasn't cheap,
Not when Dad's wage was fifty bob
And he thought his was a well paid job!
Our house had all that one could have,
Gas, running water and a lav',
Though some did have electric lights
We lit gas mantles on dark nights.
Our lav' was outside in the yard
So winter evenings were quite hard,
But on bleak nights of rain and thunder
Mum let us use a tin 'gosunda'.
Looking back now, it seems so strange
How she cooked on that kitchen range;
With its oven heated by coal
That the coalman tipped down a hole
Into a grimy cellar below -
A place where no-one liked to go.
We had no fridge or washing machine -
Just Mum's hard work to keep us clean.
There was no bath - just a zinc tub
Brought indoors for your weekly scrub.
The 'Great Unwashed' they call us now
Though we tried our best anyhow;
Life was rough and tough in most ways -
Still they remain my happiest days,
But isn't it a constant truth
That the same applies to most people's youth?

A F Allen

UNTITLED

Last night Dad at the stroke of
twelve, rolled home drunk as a lord
in hell. He'd spent all day in the
Old Red Forge spending the last of
the week's Lloyd George. Mum, as usual, to
make ends meet would cook for madam at
her late night treat. Half a crown I
think she got, but believe me, then
that bought a lot.

And sometimes madam, a kindly soul with
three young children of her own, would
send for us a large portmanteau, brimmed with joy
and goodies as bright as Santa's stocking on the
night of nights.

Excitement shook our hands with pleasure
as we shared each single treasure, embracing
every tiny thing so that even now my
heart still sings with memories sweet
of the way we were.

My God! My mother had a heart of gold
and a will of shimmering steel!

She feared none, not even Adolf with
his shells and bombs and his evil snatching of
her only sons, and the black, black nights with
blacker skies when the
sirens moaned to tear-filled eyes.

And she suffered. By God, she suffered!
But she never gave in . . .
And the wonder is it's life this minute that
glows with the joy of the past that's in it.

Daisy Arkwright

TIMES PAST

Sometimes I have a longing, for what has
                            long-since past
When life was at a gentle pace
                            and didn't go so fast
When people would acknowledge you
                            and pass the time of day
Instead of which they all rush by
                            and tell you they can't stay

You'd take the children off to school and chat
                            as you walked along
But now it's shove them in the car
                            in case they take too long
You'd call upon your neighbour
                            and have a cup of tea
You can't do that now anymore
                            there's far too much to see

For the hub of life you went along
                            to the local village shop
The supermarket's quicker now
                            in the rush that must not stop
You'd take time to cook both cakes and pies
                            on what was 'baking day'
All the food is instant now
                            or from the take-away

For a holiday you went out of town
                            to a tent or caravan
And travelled down there on the train
                            or in a charabanc
Holidays now are a different thing
                            you have to fly abroad
And go and lay down in the sun
                            to somewhere you can't afford

A lengthy letter from a friend
                         would keep you up to date
You quickly now pick up the phone
                         in case you're running late
Reflecting back life seemed so good
                         when you had the time of day
But sadly now we have to say
                         that speed is here to stay

Elizabeth Walker

CHEERFUL DAYS!

Happier the way we were, no discontent
Providing we could pay the rent,
Loaned a 'bob' 'til end of week
To neighbours whose further meals looked bleak.

Friday pay days; Thursday's dinner ever egg,
Boiled, served with soldier's bread,
The treat of steak or chop next day,
Good food expense, good health mainstay.

Neighbours helped each other, payment never sought,
Labour given, none looked for aught,
But would be returned someday
When two pairs of hands needed some way.

Everyone smiled, roundsmen tunefully whistled,
Usual, no-one bristled,
A camaraderie was taught,
Support each other and dread nought.

Children played in street, when a race was begun,
At line-up mothers joined in fun.
Nights, yarns of parents when young,
Worse times, good firm friends they lived among.

Contented, cheerful although short of money,
Small treats made world sunny,
Picnics, bus rides, cakes a delight,
Learned economics overnight.

Our time's blessings, tap dancing, jazz band swingers,
Coppers for baths and laundry wringers!
False 'choppers', tombstone humdingers,
Films, love tales, Westerns, gang gunslingers.

Hilary Jill Robson

'IN THE GOOD OLD, BAD OLD DAYS...'

Do you recall the musicals?
A swear word never heard!
When men were men and girls were girls -
Such things are best preferred!
The flicks were worth their weight in gold
And stars were really stars!
Our heroes stood their ground, so bold,
And proudly bore their scars!
We watched enthralled, engaged, engrossed -
Their exploits touched our hearts . . .
In fact, it was no idle boast,
Our idols played their parts!
We'll never see their like again -
They really set the tone . . .
I'd score them all: ten out of ten -
The best we've ever known!
They made us laugh, they made us cry,
They taught us truths to trust . . .
They made us think . . . to question why
Some things were not discussed . . .
If only films were like they were -
They had a touch of class!
But now, they're just a flash, a blur . . .
They're nothing but a farce . . .
Thank God I've got a video
To play them once again!
Yes, every night another show -
Great films when men were men!

Denis Martindale

All Our Yesterdays

We grew up together, two Liverpool kids
In a street not far from the docks,
The streets were our playground, and our beach
Was the Cast Iron Shore filled with rocks.

The tuppenny rush at the Palace flicks
Was the highlight of the week,
We cheered the goodies, booed the baddies
And tried not to get shoved off the seat.

There was no lack of work to bother us,
Opportunities were so many,
We lived back in those halcyon days
When jobs were ten-a-penny.

We watched the rejoicing on VE night
Of thousands round St George's Hall,
The uniforms of many nations
Joined together in the victory ball.

Then came swinging skirts, wasp-waist belts,
Bobbysocks and trews,
Beehive hairstyles, black-rimmed eyes
And winkle-picker shoes.

And oh, how we danced at the local hop,
The beat of the music was great
We jitterbugged, jived and bopped around
With the teddy boys in their drapes.

When we're together we roll back the years
And laugh at the things we did,
Affection and friendship still live on today
As when we were a couple of kids.

F Gerrard

TODAY OR YESTERDAY - WHICH IS REALLY ADVANCED?

Fast cars, computer games, girl power
The world of technology grows by the hour.
A ring of the microwave signals dinner is ready
Then it's out on the town
Who wants to go steady?

Home from school,
Mother is baking.
From a hard day's work,
Father is aching.
Families gathered, sharing their news
Listening with respect to grandparents' views.

Late night shopping, heavy traffic
Through the aisles we dash.
Saturday evening, it's Mystic Meg
Who will win the cash?

Carefree children playing marbles, hopscotch on the street
'Don't stay out too long. Beware of strange men you meet.'
'Please Mum, I'll get picked on.
Everyone else has those trainers in my class.'
Best clothes pressed and ready
To wear for Sunday Mass.

Liberation, great gadgets
No strict Victorian values, people may say
But take me back to those treasured moments
Clean, simple living any day!

Helen Georgeou

1940's GRAMMAR SCHOOL

'A miner's child a grammar school pupil?'
She first must gain a scholarship entrance.
To buy a place would cost too much money;
If earned she would appreciate success.
Determined stand could help her to get there
By study and parents' sacrifices.

She passed and, grateful she had achieved this,
Wore her school uniform with much delight.
She practised through life the conduct they taught;
Respect for other people's opinions,
Discussion without provoking anger,
To keep learning processes evergreen.

From time to time orchestral visitors
Encouraged love of classical music;
Because teachers taught her not to do so,
She never imposed her tastes upon all.
Improvements in her knowledge of English
Included basic rules of poetry.

There she received a grounding in Latin,
Which helped her in quite unexpected ways,
To understand words and derivations,
Thus comprehending language construction.
She learned of facts that she'd never thought of
And stored them up for future reference.

The parquet floors in school shone so brightly;
So not to deface them, she wore soft house shoes.
She gained the need to contemplate beauty,
To care how her deeds affected others,
Because she valued their approbation,
She endeavoured much to please her parents.

Joan Knight

Play Rock 'n' Roll For Me

Chorus Play rock 'n' roll for me,
And let The King sing.
Let's recall what used to be,
Before our dreams went tumbling.

I was a fifties' menace,
Never had no time for schools.
An engineer's apprentice
With greasy hands and tools.

But at night I'd wear my gear,
The DA, the drainies, the drape.
We'd jive down at the dance hall
On suede shoes thick with crepe.

I took you home on the last bus,
And I turned up at church the next day.
Your family didn't like us,
And tried to turn you away.

But I got an old Austin Seven,
And in that, and the back of the flicks,
We found our own kind of heaven,
Deep kissing, and Player's Number Six.

And then one day we were older,
Our youth and our dreams they had gone.
We were the next generation,
And only the music played on.

Roger J Gould

HOLDING MY BREATH

I want you to remember
my Sunday dinners.
I want you to remember,
how beautiful you are.

I want you to remember
us reading, together.
I want you to remember
I sometimes made you laugh.

I want you to remember
you steal nothing from me
but my trust.
I want you to remember
what a fool you are.

I want you to remember
that everything done for me,
you did for yourself,
as the first thought.

I want you to remember
when you take a hammer
to a piece of nature,
you get flints in your eyes
instead.

I want you to remember,
if there is no one on Earth
who can trust you,
there is no-one on this Earth,
you can trust.

I want you to remember
we can all change.
I want you to remember
That one day, I might.

Susan Roberts

THE WAY WE WERE IN WARTIME

It was open house in our air raid shelter.
At the first wailing alarm they came,
Adults half-dressed, courting couples, helter-skelter,
Dogs, cats, kids pell-mell for the wartime Noah's Ark.

Among the Thermos flasks and sandwiches we cowered,
False hilarity stilled when the droning started overhead,
The whistle of the bomb as the deadly impact roared.
Not for us this time, but next time?

People queued for hours, not for cod or lobster,
But a chunk of conger eel perhaps, or worse,
Something sinister wrapped in newspaper.
Food and the thought of food ruled our lives.

We little knew then the spartan ration book
With its meagre portions of butter, tea and sugar
Meant fitness, though a constant challenge to the cook.
Rationing, not fads and diets, trimmed the fat.

After dark air raid wardens combed the town
For cracks and chinks of betraying light.
Their imperative door-rapping a familiar sound,
While on the roofs the stoic fire-fighters kept their vigil.

Pulling together with cheerful camaraderie -
That was the way we were in wartime.

Ellen W Worthington

THE HUNGRY THIRTIES

The good old days, I wonder. We did not need to lock.
   But those in stress knocked on your door for food from your
   small stock.
No cars raced through our quiet streets. Pollution scares were low,
   And milk was served in milking shops, for penny a glass, you know.

The baker had his trotting mare, she was a pretty sight.
   And well looked after I recall, although looked just a mite.
Ice cream sold from carts that shone, we bought if funds allowed.
   But many a family had no work, the times were very hard.

The doctor's waiting room was full, the TB was well-known.
   The 'Panel list' to cover costs, with many a soul sent home.
The picture shows drew all the crowds, nine coppers took you in
   With Shirley Temple and a dog gave many a face a grin.

To get a job was all you thought, the dole queues reached the sky.
   Four million men on one last count, with little help from high.
The war declared for Poland's sake gave jobs to those in need.
   The young men's cries were met once more within a conflict's creed.

We saw it through and looking back we hope it was worthwhile.
   The sadness borne, the friendships won from years of toil and trial.

Joan G Railiffe

REMEMBER?

Fluffy clouds, ships at anchor
The widest bay,
Are you calling me
Across the spray?

When you set sail
And lift the anchor
Shall I remember you
Far away?

Nostalgic feelings overpower me
And sends you on your way
Takes me back to our first endeavour
Do you remember?

Tangling tow ropes, a sail set free
Guiding gently o'er the sea.
Now night is falling, shadows flee
Only the moonlight and me.

Joan Hands

Only The Old . . .

Now I am old, I remember
The good things in my early life,
The peace in our own little village,
Where everyone lived without strife.

The highways with so little traffic,
The meadows bedecked with wildflowers,
The mushrooms just there for the picking,
The stream, unpolluted, was ours.

And home, with its oil lamps and candles,
The kitchen range, glowing so red,
The hip-bath beside it for comfort,
An oven-warmed brick in the bed.

Amusements home-made and invented,
And sometimes, a rare little treat,
A trip to the pictures for sixpence,
Or the gramophone tempting our feet!

The village shop had all we needed,
And much more to make children stare,
Kali-suckers, gob-stoppers and liquorice,
For those with a penny to spare.

The smithy was quite an attraction,
Or the steam roller smoothing the street,
The 'Bobby', well-known and respected,
And feared, as he plodded his beat.

Only the old can remember
The good things of those early years,
So simple, but treasured forever,
And only their loss causes tears.

Joan Letts

THE GOOD OLD DAYS

Don't talk to me about the good old days
When poverty and hunger were rife
When the top wage a week was four pounds ten
To keep a man children and wife

The rent for a two-up and two-down house
Was twelve shillings and six pence a week
And the coal and gas were about the same
Meant that money for food was quite bleak

Just three pounds five shillings for clothing and food
And we had nine mouths to be fed
My mum often scrubbed the butcher's shop floor
To earn for our dinner a sheep's head

No holidays at all no trips on the bus
And a two mile walk to the park
Where there were swings and roundabouts that you had to push
And a ha'poth of sweets was your mark

In 1926 came the general strike
And for weeks no one got any pay
If you were like us and went hungry to bed
You got down on your knees to pray

I was by now helping out with the funds
A butcher's delivery boy at 12 years of age
But although I had passed the 11+ exam
We couldn't afford the school blazer of beige

Twelve hours per week at two hours per day
One hour before and one after school
Six days a week for the princely pay
And six shillings a week was the rule

The good old days did I hear you say
Then the war took my youth and threw it away

Hubert Hayes

BARE FACTS

Concrete floors
and bare-wood tables
Bricky-boiler built into wall,
Stoke that fire - any old rubbish
Keep the laundry on the boil.
Poss 'em - scrub 'em
Use some soda
Barrel-tub and wringing machine,
No 'smelly softener' - no fancy powder -
Elbow-grease will make 'em clean.
Pennorth o' bones please
At the butcher's
'For the dog sir - if you please'
Bones with any veg available
Made a family's daily meal.
In the winter
Dark nights falling
Call of nature
We braved the storm,
Down the yard -
Each family member
Following on
While the seat was warm.
No electric - the odd gas-fitting,
Buy a mantle - clip it on,
Flimsy gauze - careful - it's fragile
Dammit all! Another thruppence gone!

Mary Skelton

Grandma's Photo Album

Come closer dear, I can't hear you,
Bring the album and open it wide:
That's your grandpa in the hay cart
With a pitch fork by his side.

There is Bonnie, gentle giant,
And those are brasses shining bright:
This, a picnic in the hayfield
Rover pleading for a bite.

Home-baked bread in wicker baskets,
Scalding tea in enamel jug,
Cider poured from shoulder flagon
Into cow horn, not a mug.

Shires between the shafts awaiting
In scented fields of sun-dried hay,
Farmhands loading creaking wagons
Pitching high to fill the bay.

Children playing by the haystacks
Hide-and-seek, a favourite game,
Begging rides on patient Bonnie
And for rides in empty wain.

Sun was then forever shining,
Panama hats seen everywhere,
Youngsters' feet were thrust in plimsolls
Legs, when not in lisle, were bare.

That's enough now, hush your questions
And let your grandma have her sleep:
Store the album in the sideboard
Memories will always keep.

N M Beddoes

'NEW' FOR 'OLD'

I was looking forward to life in ''39,
When the bombshell dropped at radio time.
I had always been told wartime days were over,
I was lucky to live in days of 'clover'.

That still remains true, I'm lucky to be here,
Life is special, but the cost was dear.
Rations and the loss of many friends,
Still leave a mark when wartime ends.

The good days to me are in '98,
When I hope all will learn not to 'hate'.
Lots of problems to overcome,
But with hope, work and faith it will be done.

Forget the so-called 'Good Old Days'
There's so much to live for in many ways.
Life for all could be much worse,
Put the 'Good *new* days' first.

Cindy White

SISTERS GOING TO THE PETTY

Rushing out into the cold dark night
down the path without a light,
feeling for the sneck on the door,
slipping on the icy floor
waiting for the hinge to creak
pushing it wide with our feet.
Crossing our legs, this was a race.
Feeling our way in the dark space
to find the double wooden seat
and spend a penny so to speak.
Eyes accustomed to whitewashed walls
pulling down our navy smalls.
Sighing, we found relief alone,
was that someone walking over stone?
Sounds of crunching boots came ever near.
Together, sitting huddled up in fear
as candlelight cast shadows on the wall
of Father's image like a giant tall,
to lead us back to a cosy kitchen fire
away from this cold outside mire.

Jean Sweeney

I Remember Stanley

Now I remember Stanley, from when I were a lad
The things we got up to you could not call bad
Slightly mischievous,
Naughty perhaps,
But we never did harm, it was all just for laughs.
We would tie up the door knockers on Canalside Row
With a length of cotton and then we would go,
To hide in the hedge
Then pull on the string
Like five ghosts a-knocking, is there anyone in.
We'd go scrumping for apples, that is Stanley and I
We stay out to midnight, or till the bobby passed by
I felt so free
Not a care in my heart
Isn't it funny how it all falls apart.
I saw Stanley the other day, no longer a lad,
His grandchildren had visited, of this he was glad.
Now he stays in the house
Afraid to go out,
Since the kids, just for fun, chose to push him about.
They stole Stanley's wallet, and blackened his eye,
All of the time he just pleaded out why.
I do not understand,
I really don't know,
What happened to the good times of so long ago.

R Chapman

THE WAY WE WERE

In times remembered long ago
   when life seemed quieter and slow,
I used to sit sometimes at night
   to see the twinkling stars so bright.
But now, where have they all gone?
   You are lucky to see just one.
We children to the park would ride
   on scooters that were so tried!
Under the mat our front door key
   for thirty years it used to be.
Until the last war when we left
   like many others to the west.
Ration books, identity cards, sugarless tea
   a military tailor worked for me!
Sadly, I used to meet young men
   who would wear those uniforms and then
Off to fight, or fly a plane,
   so many never to come back again.
Depending on the life one had
   old days mixed with good and bad,
So pray in the coming millennium year,
   our lives will find a pathway clear.

Alice M Archer

THE WAY WE WERE

Remember when I have asked myself why?
As I did not want to remember all it would imply.
But as the stress of the 90's got to me
I look back at the 60's when I felt free.
The world had not the fast pace of this present life
You did not fear the madman with a knife.
Trust and peace were all around
Qualities today of which are difficult to be found.
Meals tasted like real food
With no additives to make you in a mood
Life was just so pleasant, although the money was short.
But nothing compared to the 90's,
How we now feel so fraught.

Jean Rendell

REFLECTIONS

Oh! where are my friends from my service days?
Where are the girls I knew?
Do they think of me as I think of them?
If only that I knew.

A great little band, the best in the land,
Part of a happy team;
Who worked together, in every weather,
Of them I often dream.

Memory's picture of the predictor,
Suffused by colours clear,
Is imprinted on the screen of my mind,
With friends brought ever near.

Molly and Ria, they went overseas,
To mention only two,
And I landed down in dear London Town,
To meet the start of V-2.

Those war scarred years they brought laughter and tears;
Some lives were torn apart,
Others may see the millennium years:
Thanks to a good stout heart.

But where are my friends from my service days?
Where are the girls I knew?
One misses them most in the twilight years,
Perhaps they miss me too?

Margaret Knox Stubbs

THE GOOD OLD DAYS

The good old days they really were,
When we all seemed to be without a care.
No rushing around in a mad busy world,
Time to watch the beauty of a flower unfurled.

No roaring of traffic and its harsh sounds,
When you could see so much to be bought with a pound,
You walked to school all on your own,
No fear of abduction, such things were unknown.

With a penny in your hand for a sherbet dip,
Even a gobstopper or a liquorice stick,
You went to the corner shop to get a loaf for your mum,
Then walked home again in the lovely sun.

It was never sliced, in fact you nibbled a bit,
And hoped they didn't notice or you may get the stick,
We didn't have much money but they were happy days,
There were whips and tops and hopscotch to play.

You were taught dancing, maybe ballet and tap,
Such lovely times what could be better than that,
You were taught manners, morals, how not to go astray,
Yes they surely were the good old days.

Barbara Ann Barker

Way Back Then

I often sit and ponder
Of the days that used to be,
Living in the country,
Holidays beside the sea.

Living in a small village
We seldom saw a stranger,
Wandered through the hills and lanes
Without a thought of danger.

Easter was a happy time
On the hills we used to roam,
Have a picnic and a sing-song
Then saunter tired and happy home.

We had a seaside holiday
The donkey ride was grand,
We asked for nothing more
But castles made of sand.

For the village bonfire
A guy was always made
And all around the streets
There was a small parade.

There would be roasted chestnuts
And potatoes baked a treat,
Plenty there for everyone,
Toffee apples for a sweet.

At Christmas we picked holly
While walking on the hills,
Made our own paper chains
And all the little frills.

Life was much more simpler then
Or so it seems to me,
Now there's always too much rush
And no time just to be.

B C Watts

I Remember

I remember - when my parents had a hairdressing salon
From 8 till 8, Dad was busy, with haircuts and shaves
Mum worked in the back room - with a side entrance to the street
Styling ladies' hair - with setting and marcel waves.

With my brother and sister - we all lived over the shop
In small rooms - with the only 'loo' out in the back yard
In summertime - 'paying a visit' - was no problem at all
But, in cold winter - brr - venturing out there - was certainly hard.

I remember - that mile long walk to school, every day
Why - I even walked home and back for lunch
And those schoolboy fights - when I thought I was 'top dog'
Until - some novice - threw a lucky punch.

I remember - the value of the old halfpenny
It bought a bag of sweets - to last all day
And the only vandalism, we could be accused of
Was knocking at someone's door - then - running away.

I remember - going to that fleapit - we called 'The Pictures'
Every Saturday morn - we all hated the villain - we would boo and hiss
And I remember - little Annie - who smiled so sweetly
And shyly confessed I was the first boy - she had ever kissed

I remember - the Jarrow hunger marchers - and Edward's abdication
I remember - Chamberlain's piece of paper - and Sir Oswald Mosley's 'black shirts'
I remember - yesterdays world, - and its many happenings
I remember - the sound of laughter - the joys - and the hurts.

Paul Gold

SUBURBAN ALMANAC OF THE THIRTIES

While Ramsey MacDonald strained to halt
Wild inflation - and calm the economy,
Martinis and champagne dwindled into
Beer and sherry for the people, by default.
Future nerves drove them to postpone bonhomie,
Till they'd made an appliance-buying coup.

London Transport saw fit to extend
Underground connections to the suburbs.
Many of its business staff went home
There, when office-working days would end.
Thus, rail service promised to be superb,
Tempting them to set up house, or roam

Beyond the system, in quest of the nest
Of wedded bliss in areas evolving,
Photographed and advertised by agents.
New estates claimed assets that might best
Attract house-hunting families - involving
Walking-minutes distance from the stations.

Modernistic cinema facades
Of concrete or glass, were staunchly real;
But interiors cared for illusions.
From expensive seats, or semi-hard
Cheaper ones, (subtracting comfort from the deal,)
Hopes and dreams came outside - to be delusions.

Gillian C Fisher

THE HALFPENNY TRAM

Life was so simple then: a trip up town on the halfpenny tram;
my brother and me and our Dad and Mam.
Faces scrubbed: shoes a shine: two pennies clasped tightly in
excited hands: Mam in her Sunday frock: a lock of hair escaping
from her best hat: Dad in his starched collar and fancy vest.
A trip to Hull market was a Saturday treat: striped awnings: clattering
feet on worn cobble stones: neat pats of butter in greaseproof coats;
freshly baked bread warm from the oven: plump juicy oranges
sixpence a dozen.
Sherbet dips that made our eyes water: liquorice allsorts a penny
a quarter: round shiny gobstoppers a farthing each: patty and chips or
a soft downy peach.
The toy stall was magic with so many delights: we could choose a whip
and a top or a painted gold kite; there was cut-out dollies a bat and
a ball: a clown on a stick or transfers to lick.
Shop at my stall called the butchers and bakers: roll-up for bargains;
will there by any takers?
Then baskets full and pennies spent we rode back home on the teatime
tram.
Me: my brother: our Dad and our Mam.

Chris Senior

THE GOOD OLD DAYS

Years ago before the car, people didn't travel far.
A walk to the shops, or a trip to the park
And there weren't many people out after dark.
The men would go for a pint up the pub,
But the women stayed home, to cook the grub.
The children were safe playing in the street,
Some wore shoes and some had bare feet.
One the Sabbath they all wore their Sunday best
And went to church along with the rest.
Coal or log fires, were their only source of heat
And you always saw a 'bobby', walking the beat.
No washing machines, or fitted carpets on the floor
And nobody ever had to lock their door.
Families were very close and set in their ways,
But then after all, those were the good old days.

G Silver

MY FAMILY
(The past is another country; they do things differently there)

The family was different then -
No child-support, no governmental grants;
A family was made of parents, children,
Their parents, (and grandparents), uncles, aunts.

My family was thus: of several generations,
Most relatives unscathed by recent strife;
I knew those nearest, parents and grandparents,
They were the background that informed my life.

The family was headed by my father,
Large, solid, but irascible; secure;
He ruled the household roost, made the decisions,
Inspired with terror, though his love was sure.

My mother stayed at home, as was the custom,
Obeyed resentfully her generation's laws;
She cooked the meals, she did the hated dusting,
Bequeathed to me dislike of household chores.

I knew their fathers, and my father's mother,
They all conspired to spoil me, or constrain;
They influenced my growing, formed my values,
Showed me a world that cannot come again.

And so I am that thing despised of all men,
Beneath contempt, wherever I may pass,
Betrayed by accent, attitudes and values:
I know my sin - I'm purely middle class.

Elizabeth Parish

NOSTALGIA

Do you remember Christmases with home-made paper chains,
And winters when it always snowed and we all had chilblains,
Hot water bottles in the bed and blankets all a-heap,
And still we shivered in our vests until we fell asleep.

I'd quite forgotten chilblains and the icy draught that blew
Under the door and up our backs chilling us right through,
While huddling round a roaring fire, our shins and faces toasted,
And watching chestnuts blacken in the skillet as they roasted.

Do you remember larders - not the box-like motor cars,
But cupboards off the kitchen stacked with packages and jars,
A marble slab for cheeses and another one for meats,
And coloured tins with pictures on for home-baked cakes and treats.

Lisle stockings were the thing to wear when I was at High School,
Suspender belts and bodices - no chance of acting 'cool'.
In winter there were fleecy drawers beneath a pleated gymslip,
And woe betide the girl who wore a decorated hairgrip!

Remember massive ledgers that were written out in ink,
With columns that were totted up in less than half a wink?
Pounds, shillings, pence we had to add pre-decimalisation.
No need for electronics for that simple calculation.

I wonder what became of that material called crimplene?
I'd dresses, coats and trouser suits all made on my machine.
So easy to keep fresh and smart - just wear and wash and wear.
They kept their shape and colour with the minimum of care.

So many things have come and gone, and some of them are missed,
But there are far more changes for the better I could list.
So while I sometimes reminisce about 'the good old days'
My life today is easier in many different ways.
Inventions and technology have helped us all somehow,
And I am pleased that *then* was then and I am living *now!*

Patricia Farley

THE WAY WE WERE

We didn't have a bathroom,
But had baths every week -
Standing in a 'dolly tub'
And came out clean and sleek!

We had an outside toilet,
A building near the house,
And though our home was spotless -
We sometimes saw a mouse!

We listened to the wireless
For news and stories too, -
Went to church and Sunday school
But clothes were rarely new!

Our mother told us stories
About her childhood days
As we made our teatime toast -
Or helped in other ways!

Neighbours helped each other out,
When trouble came their way,
In the war we found out too -
How everyone would pray

Our farmers and our land girls,
Provided healthy food,
Loved ones sent away to war
To fight for other's good!

I look back with pleasure now,
Upon my childhood days,
Memories of those dearest friends,
Stay in a golden haze!

Marguerite Brassington-Griffiths

Untitled

My love spared, as is my life,
From this hell on earth.
This war's now passing,
and the good lord noting, my worth.

With these blood-red fields of spring,
only he knows what tomorrow brings.
Maybe my soul will be spared,
be left to see another dawn.
I pray to thy lord, help me back home,
to my family forever more.

Raymond John Mandeville

THE LANE

As I get older my thoughts often go
Back to the lane where I lived long ago.
Last house on the right - the one back to back
Where the lane petered out and became just a track.
The track to the fields where we used to play.
Never dreaming that they would be built on one day.
I remember a den that we built amongst trees
And father's allotment where I went to 'pinch' peas.
We also kept hens, the old one was no fool.
She knew just the right time to meet me from school.
One particular day, I recall with delight
Allowed to be first to switch on the light.
For 'electric' had come to our cosy backwater.
With ceremonial 'switch-on' performed by young daughter.
Bath time for all was a weekly event.
Friday night by the fire in tin bath with a dent.
Trips into town on the buses so few
If you missed the 11 you waited 'til two.
Playmates were rare - it was usually the cat.
But I never found anything strange about that.
As a young lady it began to seem dull
It didn't quite seem to fill life to the full.
So I moved to the town to see the bright lights
To shopping - filled days and party-filled nights.
But as I grow older my thoughts often go
To the peace of the lane where I lived along ago.

Gwenneth Woodall

GRANDMA'S MEMORIES
(Dedicated to my grandma - Kathleen Hicks)

Grandma remembers those bygone days
and often a tear fills her eye.
Her memories crisp and crystal clear
Of all of the time that's passed by.
She remembers the times as a little girl,
the simple freedom of play.
She remembers the times spent away from home,
Serving others as part of her day.
Cooking, and cleaning the master's house
Yet herself she was only a child.
Though hard she worked at her daily chores,
In her mind she's in fields running wild.

Fond memories through all of her life,
Of all of the years that she spent,
Caring for all of her family
and she wonders where all of it went.
She does not need photos or diaries,
to remember the things that she's done.
In her mind the pictures are crisp and clear,
in her head, her past still lives on.
So I watch as grandma remembers.
As a new tear springs to her eye.
And I'm glad she'll be part of my memories.
Always there as the years pass me by.

Tracy Howie

SONG OF THE SHIRT
(To be sung while ironing)

Oh I yearn
to return
    to Zambezi,
to the shores
where the chores
    are made easy.
There dirt
on a shirt
    never matters -
clothes torn,
or forlorn,
    or in tatters.

To wash
or look posh
    is a vice,
though to strip
for a dip
    can be nice.
If my togs
in the bogs
have been smeared,
I effect
self-respect
    by my beard.

I can bake
a plain cake
    in the sun,
and brew
white ant stew
    just for fun.

Oh . . . back
in my shack
   life is easy;
how I yearn
to return
   dear Zambezi!

Wyn Cornish

THE WAY WE WERE

Simple pleasures appreciated in full measure
Memories we now treasure
No locking of doors or piles of junk post
A cup of tea come share it with me
Bacon two shillings, it would be
A joint of beef 2/6d to be paid
What was left from Sunday
Was minced on Monday.
No fancy clothes, couldn't afford those
A hard-boiled egg a Sunday pleasure.
The outside privy newspaper on a string
Toilet rolls weren't the going thing.
Evening pastime, spent at the flicks
A penny bag of sweets what a treat.
Supper time penny bag chips, with plenty of crispy bits,
And vinegar supplied, that did the trick

Joan Patrickson

Happy Days

I remember the days so clear
We could play outside
But stayed near
Those were the happy days
Before war came along
We had to go to places
Where we did not belong
But I loved the countryside
The farms and the fresh air
Those were the happy days
But war was ahead
I was not frightened
I had a cosy bed
They bombed most of London
Coventry as well
Mothers worked in factories
Men fought like hell

Our house was still standing
But oh what a mess
Other people lost their homes
Some did their best
But peace was coming to us
Happy days were due
Let us live peacefully
Happy days for me and you

P M Wardle

THE GOOD OLD DAYS

Give me the good old days
where time passed slowly by.
When I used to speak to Grandma
when I was just a boy.
In the summer hols
we would go with Mam,
and take the young ones in the pram.
Pea picking, fruit picking,
potatoes and hops.
We were deep in the countryside,
away from the shops.
We would take wood from hedgerows
and make us a fire,
boil up the kettle and
sit down awhile.
The smell from the bacon,
and taste of the tea,
sat around the camp fire
are now memories to me.

John Hickman

THE EVACUEES

I was a London evacuee on October 1939.
Luckily the weather was fine.
Marched single file, two by two,
from Lollard Street to Waterloo.
With our square-boxed gas mask and suitcase,
we were hurried along, no time to waste.
Teachers and helpers kept an eye
on the procession as it went by.
Each had a label tied to our coats
like a parcel just put in the post.
Our destination was somewhere in Devon.
There were children there as young as seven.
We got in our seats, goodbyes were said.
Would I ever again see my old bed?
Some were crying, some silent, the mood elation.
Whistle blew, the train pulled out of the station.
Then came the feeling of utter despair.
What was to happen? Did anyone care?
Why were we leaving? Would we be all right?
I was a child of nine and numb with fright.
No idea of politics or impending war.
Could only react to what I saw.
Tugs of emotion and holding back tears,
those long ago children expressing their fears.
I was not to know that after church on Sunday,
war would be declared and end any fun day.

Ann May Wallace

TEA RATIONS

We're having a family gathering, me auntie's come to tea
She's brought me cousin Malcolm so there's me brother, him and me

We've been to see the rabbit and poked a carrot through the door
We looked for eggs amongst the hens but there just aren't any more

We think we might play cricket but we can't find a proper ball
We've rolled a piece of 'Echo up, but it doesn't work at all.

The grown ups are talking private - they've got a lot to say
They don't want us three listening in, so we've been sent out to play.

Me Mother says when grown ups talk, we mustn't say a word
She says, in fact, that children should be seen but never heard.

I like me Auntie Hilda 'cos she's always got a smile
She sings, 'She'll be coming round the mountain' - In fact she sings it
                                                                          all the while!

But today she's talking to our Mum, she wants to ask a favour
She says, 'What a lovely cup of tea it's got a lovely flavour.'

'This rationing really gets me down I know you must agree
Now - do you think you could oblige me with a packet or two of tea?'

'We get a skinny bit of margarine, half an egg just now and then
The last time I saw biscuits - well, I can't remember when!'

'But it's *tea* I miss the most of all, the taste I can't forget
If you could spare a quarter I'd be forever in your debt.'

So me auntie and our Malcolm toddle off catch their bus
A cup of tea! She must be mad what's all the bloomin' fuss?

If I was me auntie Hilda I know what I'd choose for me
It'd be dandelion and burdock - not a flippin' cup of tea!

Pam Quigley

WHEN GRAN WAS YOUNG

When I was just a little girl I used to stay with Gran,
She'd tell me of the way she lived when she was very young,
She didn't have a fine big house with lights and indoor loos
She went to bed by candlelight and washed in big round bowls,
She'd sit beside a big black range with heavy oven doors
Where Mum baked bread and cooked the meals and dried most of
                                                    the clothes,
Their water came from village pumps and was carried to the door
It didn't come through long thin pipes which came through
under floors,
The little building down the street was where she went to school
With Sunday school, and church on Sundays was the general rule,
She wore fine bonnets on her head, her skirts were to the floor,
And on her feet high leather boots many buttons to the fore,
They didn't have a motor car or ride around in buses
They rode around in carriages drawn by fine black horses,
They didn't have a video, computer or satellite TV,
Their toys were of the simple kind and playing games was free,
Gran lived a very simple life when she lived in the past
She wouldn't be a child today as the pace is much too fast.

Jean Roslyn Carr

REMINISCENCE

Policeman on his push bike, no 'Panda' cars back then,
It's true there were no vandals, but I remember when
Schooldays seemed such happy times, the teachers got respect
If we ever misbehaved ourselves, we knew what to expect.
Ration books and gas masks, now seem so far away
But discipline was evident, if we erred along the way.
Saturday morning pictures, a treat if we did well
'Don Winslow' of the navy, 'Lone Ranger's famous yell.
Dried egg to make an omelette, the butcher's lovely dripping
All devoured quite lovingly, at one full family sitting.
Silver paper dropped by aircraft, we often wondered why
Something to do with radio, or transmissions by a spy.
We were at war with Hitler, but 'Winnie' did us proud
On VE a party, with such a jolly crowd.
Chocolate cakes and jellies, things we had long forgot
Even apple dumplings, crisp and steaming hot.
Ice cream was then a rarity, but we had some of that
Singing songs and dressing up, each with a paper hat.
We lived out in the country, the hills and dales to roam
No worries for our parents, before dark - safely home.
Newspapers cost a 'penny', a bottle of beer a 'bob'
Run errands for the neighbours, a 'tanner' - price per job.
Now looking back, reflecting - life we had was great
Sometimes when cash was rather short, we put it 'on the slate'.
Honesty and hard work, or something overheard
Trust was at a premium - a man good as his word!

T G Bloodworth

PASSING DAYS

Give me the canvas, I will recreate
Scenes from memory. I see the names
Of London streets whose lampposts were
The hitching post for our cowboy games,
The row of houses where every door was known,
Each pavement crack counted on the way home.

The known world was our guardian then,
Not a place of strangers who might cause pain,
But a young miscreant could expect
A parental smack or the threat of the cane.
Evenings meant Children's Hour, games on the rug,
Cold bedrooms, warm beds and a big goodnight hug.

The local park was a wondrous place,
Boating lake, maze, sandpits and swings.
Then a penny to spend called for much haste,
Off to the sweet shop on feet that had wings.
Brandy balls, sherbet dabs, nougat in bars,
Endless choice waited in rows of glass jars.

Time passed and the joy of romance worked its charm.
Ahead stretched an enticing path;
But it meant up at six, strip the bed,
Shake the mattress, downstairs to shovel the ash from the hearth.
Re-lay the fire with the coarse nutty slack,
Outside in the gloom, fill the hod, tote it back.

Porridge like witches' brew bubbled for breakfast,
Bustle and scramble of boots, scarves and coats.
Afterwards, silence, but washday awaited,
The copper to fill and its low fire to coax.
I loved that old world, so safe and so slow,
But today's world has moved on, it has to be so.

Joan Hawkes

WORDS ON WAR

When the air raid sirens wailed out loud
Into the shelters we would crowd
Neighbours dashing, some distressed,
Some in nighties, some undressed
Yet blushes spared for you to me
For in the dark one could not see.
At length the loud all-clear would sound
Then we would traipse homeward bound,
Down darkened streets we would be led.
A cup of tea then straight to bed.
Before we went to school one task
Not to forget your own gas mask.,
Breakfast was bread with home-made jam
Or for a treat a slice of *spam,*
Whilst Mum would spend the day to bake
Lovely potato carrot cake.
To darn and mend was all the fashion
For even clothes were on the ration,
And in the woods for kindling wander
To save on coal and not to squander.
Now 'dig for victory' was the rage
Whilst flower borders were erased,
We planted spuds, sowed garden peas
And hand-hoed onions on our knees.
On Sundays we saw our Home Guard
Smartly marching to't pub yard,
And many a man did shed a tear
To find the pub was out of beer.
Yet since those days I've often thowt
We were rarely ever short of nowt.

David A Garside

THE STUFF OF DREAMS

I still remember waking in the night,
My brother standing close beside my bed.
His urgent voice - 'Come on - no time to dress!'
As Mum and Dad the worst did dread.

To me, this was a game, with nought to fear -
Our siren suits were cosy, warm and red.
To go out now, in darkest night
Into our shelter, warmed and fed.

At school, the fun - when sirens blared.
In lines precise, we filed below the ground.
To hear the stories teachers told
And sang *such* songs until the 'all clear' sound.

But we were lucky, Dad was still at home,
He grew as much food as he could.
No flowers graced the sideboard in the house,
The shelter stove took everything of wood.

Some bombs dropped close to where we lived.
The city centre died at Xmas time,
We shared the food we had with others in the street;
So many fathers died, and in their prime.

'Twas only as we grew we learned the truth,
About the horror and the shame -
That human beings can so cruel be
Each to the other - kill and maim.

Una Ellis

THE GOOD OLD DAYS

People talk about the good old days but what do they really mean?
Are they remembering their childhood or perhaps their early teens
Or when they first got married and faced life with starry eyes,
Dismissing all the hardships and the politicians' lies.
Was life always rosy, were times never fraught?
I wonder, do those good old days include the war we fought?
I suppose it's human nature to look back on life with pleasure
Remembering the good times that gave us moments we can treasure.
I wonder, will the children of today look back, reminisce in the same
                                                    sort of way?
I have happy memories of my childhood but I'm also very sure
There was still that 'big divider' some folk rich and others poor.
We were very lucky, in a certain sort of way
We had a lot more freedom than the children of today.
We'd often take a picnic not come home 'till late,
We'd not meet any weirdos, the world wasn't full of hate.
When I was young there wasn't the stress,
No plastic money your neighbours to impress.
We lived at a time when people cared and understood,
They'd listen to your troubles and help you if they could.
Now if you've a problem people would probably say
'I'll try and come round tomorrow, I'm rather busy today.'

Yvonne King

Old Hippies Never Die
(They Fade Just Like Their Dreams)

Worn like his Donna records
Gone a whiter shade of pale.
His thoughts of peace and happiness
Like himself are old and frail.
His hair band styled in Indian art
In place - though not now needed
The flowing locks it held in place
Having long ago receded
His children, Sky and Harmony
Have left him to his games
They are something in the city
And using assumed names.
In his ageing hand-stitched lifestyle
Where he weaves his dream of peace
The plants he grew in his garden
Confiscated by the police.
His wife stands in the kitchen
Making pots of rhubarb jam
Sighing 'I cook, I wash, I hoover,
I bake - therefore I am!'
Their flower-decked mini now a shed
Where free-range hens lay speckled eggs
While home-made wine - from an unknown vine
Is drunk down to the dregs
The multicoloured cares of life
Are nuts cracked with a mallet
As ageing white, and gathering dark
Are mixed up on the pallet.

Russell Adams

A Farm Called Hope

I mind from childhood a farm called 'Hope',
a four-square building that a child might draw.
Above the doorway was a limestone cope

with weathered carving and an oaken door
four steps from sunlight to the precious cool
that dairied butter on its stony floor.

The water siphoned from its earthly pool
by cast-iron handles to a deep stone sink
where farmwife balanced on a three-legg'd stool;

and oh! the purity of that cold drink.
I mind the dankness of the cellar too:
and dust-filled attics in the sunlight's blink.

A rubble pathway to the garden loo
made unsweet welcome in the summer heat -
a hut, pit, planking that was shaped for two.

I mind the pleasure of a childhood seat
on patient horses at the plodding plough,
my body bending with the hip-drop feet.

The gift of apples from the laden bough
of shape fantastic but a taste to tease.
The warm milk pumping from contented cow

to metal bucket at the farmer's knees.
The glint of sundown through the high barn door:
the smell of barley in the evening breeze

from sheaves delivered to the stubble floor
by the clanking reaper and the binding rope;
and the stooks a'drying their seductive store.

Pleasures taken granted when a child had scope
to dream of Eternity, and live in Hope.

Rebecca Pine

The Way We Were

So many things were different many years ago,
When streets were lit by lamplight and pay was very low,
Toilets in the garden so very cold and damp.
In winter when it was so dark they used a miner's lamp.
Ladies' clothes were very long, the men plus-fours did wear.
The cloth they used for making these was coarse and hard to tear.
Ration books were issued yes and gas masks too,
Should food or petrol be your want you had to join a queue.
Children had to walk to school of buses there weren't any
Then when the weekend came around were given just one penny.
But people seemed so happy then so kind in many ways,
I wonder if they really were such sad and bad old days.

I Price

STUDENTS' HOPS

When we were students long ago and went each day to college,
We took time off on Saturdays from our pursuit of knowledge
To queue for entry to the 'hop' where, suitably escorted,
We waltzed, fox-trotted, quickstepped too, or happily cavorted
In 'strip the willows', strathspeys, reels, then thirstily proceeded
Towards the café for a tea or coffee, badly needed!
But now young people dance alone with actions weird, exotic,
Their faces pale and zombie-like, their movements quite robotic!
Perhaps I'm looking at the past through rosy-tinted glasses,
But still think we had much more fun, we student lads and lasses!

Rhoda D Strath

THE WAY WE WERE

Most of the men were in the war,
A good few women too,
But you could rely on the bobby on his beat,
To keep an eye on you.

A quarter of sweets was allowed per week,
Dried egg and sometimes spam,
Or you could dig for victory
If you made a garden plan.

At Christmas you'd have a game or book,
Or even an apple and an orange,
Perhaps extra sweets from coupons saved,
And a silver sixpence in your stocking.

The teachers were strict,
And some schools were part-time,
But we learned the three'Rs',
And didn't commit major crime.

A coal fire would warm you,
And cook your toast through
While you listened to the wireless,
About Dick Barton and crew!

The seasons were more settled,
So we could plan our fun,
Like out all day in summer,
And winter snowballing to come.

Times have changed and I've one regret,
Then it was safe to play outside
For the children of my generation;
But not for today's child.

Mary McPhee

MEMORIES OF YESTERYEAR

As I sit in my soft comfortable chair
And into space I stare and stare.
My mind drifts back, memories tumble out
And I remember what yesterday was all about.

How we played games in the street
'Cause Mom wanted us out from under her feet.
I remember the rag and bone man, his old horse and cart
He'd give you a goldfish if you fetched clothes, quick sharp.
We lived in a council house, things were quite hard
Even the lavatory was out in the yard.
But neighbours were friendly, they'd chat over the wall
And they'd always be there if you felt ill at all.
With the war came rationing, food was scarce
But we seemed to manage, it could have been worse.
You had coupons for food, you know; butter, cheese and meat
Sometimes the latter would have served better on your feet.
Down on the allotment digging like mad
Planting beans and potatoes, that was my dad.
I remember the coalman with his dirty black face
Mom would count the bags as he put them in place.
But now things are different, there's central heating and such
No need for the chimney sweep with his rods and his brush.
Lavatories are inside, not outside like before
And when you leave home you double-lock your front door.
Today children play inside with computers and such
And in the way of things, seem to have too much.

I've lots of memories, I'm sure you do too
If you want to remember you know what to do.
Just make your mind blank and those memories you'll find
When you unlock the door to the storeroom of your mind.

Iris Taylor

CHRISTMAS PAST

It all seemed real when Mother
First made the Christmas cake,
And we all rushed to clean
The dish out with our spoons.
My brother went up the lane,
To get the holly and a tree
And we girls made paper chains.
We watched the snow come down
So we could get the sledge out.
There was no TV, CD, or computers
But oh how happy we were to go
Around the village singing carols.
To look forward to see what
Father Christmas had brought,
A book, a ball, a wooden top,
An apple or an orange.
To see the Nativity play,
No worry, No care, on this
      long ago Christmas Day.

R M Jeff

OVER FIFTY YEARS AGO

I can see it, even now, blue wagons loaded, high and wide
Sheaves being pitched by the farmer and the men of his employ
Grand carthorses, with me a lad, astride
Men in white Oxford shirts and trousers of corduroy
But that's over fifty years ago.

Out of school I'd rush, to help to gather in the yield
To ride the strong gentle horses, along the ripening row
In among the corn sheaves, in the harvest field
'Gee up, old fellow,' a few more strides, then 'Whoa.'
But that was over fifty years ago.

I loved those old horses, each one to me, a friend
They never asked much of life, just a field in which to sleep
But things were changing on the farm, for the horse, it was the end
No more will they the wagons pull, or the barley reap
But that was over fifty years ago.

To the field from school I came that day, eager and keen
But no horse was there, gone was Prince and Duke and the little mare
I asked where's Diamond, Short, Dumpling and Tommy, they can't
                                                                                          be seen
They've gone on a ship to a Belgium slaughterhouse somewhere
But that was over fifty years ago.

K Coleman

CHILDHOOD REVISITED

Remember when Monday was washday
and it really did take all day too?
Copper boiling, Sunlight soap, the washboard,
the rinsing, the mangling, Reckitt's blue?
Bubble and squeak for our dinner
and if lucky, for pud, spotted dick,
with lots of lovely custard that filled
you up, just the trick.

Remember Dad digging the garden
and letting us help on the plot?
The cabbages, carrots and onions
runner beans, the swedes, the shallots?
We'd all get lovely and mucky
our wellies all covered in mud.
They called it digging for victory
but it was fun digging out your own spuds.

Remember the friends we played with
all up and down the streets?
Kick the can, football, the skipping,
the hopscotch, the marbles, the sweets?
Gobstoppers that lasted forever
changing to red, green and blue
Black Jacks, lucky bags, liquorice laces,
rainbow drops, sherbet dabs, penny chews?

I look back on those days with nostalgia
those days with my mum and dad
and all of my brothers and sisters
and all of the fun we had.
The freedom to roam for miles
through fields and meadows and woods
then coming back home full of smiles.
Sadly those days are gone now for good.

J R Springthorpe

THE HORSE

I used to work down on the farm
It was many years ago
I used to work with horses
When we said 'Gee up' and 'Whoa.'

We used them on a binder
We called them Punch and Joe
They only knew one language
Wore gee, coupe gee and whoa.

'Wore gee' was for turning left
'Coupe gee' for turning right
And 'whoa' was always stopping
Especially late at night.

They always pulled the wagons
They used to pull the sweep
But now we've got the tractor
They leave bales in a heap.

You saw them pull the wedding carriage
You saw them pull the hearse
But now we've got the motor car
The roads are getting worse.

The boss he came to see us
He used a horse and trap,
And always said 'We're doing well'
Then patted us on the back.

Now when you see some horses
Just rest and think awhile
The work they used to do
It makes you want to smile.

B Salter

THIRTIES' TEENAGER

Remember the rustlings in the back row of the cinema?
The trim usherette -
'Anymore for the one and nines?'
You tried very hard -
then the daytime trysts
snatched at lunchtimes in the big city.
You worked in a gentleman's outfitters.
My steps like tramlines leading me to your store
hoping to catch a glimpse of you.
Perhaps rewarded by a wave from behind a male dummy
as you adjusted its latest fashionable clothing.
Oh that it was me
I was completely unbuttoned
and only sixteen.

Joan R Gilmour

On Sundays

On Sundays Dad was home;
The bacon ration went on Dad's plate
with 'national dried' eggs
just as yellow as yellow could be!
One Sunday the news on the BBC
said Hitler had blitzed all Coventry.

Off to Sunday School at two -
be sure to be home before blackout time.
Sunday tea beside the fire.
Mam stretched the rations to make a cake.
Then one night our house got bombed
so now I knew the meaning of war.

One Sunday Dad was gone -
called up to fight on some distant shore,
Sundays were still Sundays
only they weren't the same anymore.
At Sunday School I prayed
for my dad to come home safe from the war.

At last it was over -
no more bombs and sirens
and my dad came home to stay again.
On Sundays Dad was home
filling the chair which was empty so long
and Sundays were Sundays again.

Bea Budd

As We Were

The vast kitchen range is shining and bright
Through elbow grease and black lead
The old stone cottage is cosy and warm
With the smell of newly-baked bread

Grandma sits in a high-back chair
With always a welcoming hug
She's tearing strips from outgrown clothes
For making a bright new rug.

The jet-black kettle boils all day
On the hob by the side of the grate
Everyone's welcome, the door's never locked
No caller is ever too late.

The privy's far down the garden path
And Grandma will always explain
There's an old umbrella just by the back door
To go there in pouring rain

The copper's lit, the water's hot
And Grandma is being quite stern
The old tin bath is on the hearth
And everyone takes their turn.

No central heating, no gas, no power
We're all very warm and well fed
And go to sleep at the end of the day
In a wide deep warm feather bed!

Enid Gill

THOSE DAYS

In those days,
you felt lucky
if you got an orange
and some nuts
in your stocking at Christmas.

In those days,
you could leave
your front door unlocked
and go out
without worrying about a thing.

In those days,
you would bathe
in front of the fire
in a tub
once a week if you were lucky.

In those days,
you would walk
to school every day
in the rain
or boiling sun in summer.

(Sigh!) Whatever happened to those days?

Caz Fisher

ABOVE ALL ELSE

Today collectively we stand alone
giving all for the sake of wealth.
In the early days togetherness was all
with survival sacrificing all else.

You were innocent and I was naïve
with principles we could trust.
Speaking respectfully of them and theirs
never referring to a them and us.

A modest roof would become a home
bearing contentment hardship and pride.
And a crowded room became spacious
and welcomed whatever the size.

Good times along with violent crime
were events unique and rare.
But at least we knew what happiness was
because of our ability to care and share.

We stood defiant against the enemy
in the defence of our humble abodes.
But each household had a flexible door
which would swing from friend to foe.

And within the lining of invaluable hand-me-downs
laid a legacy only realised with time,
For today every high street brings charity home
selling a trend of what was yours is now mine.

If it's true the old days were good
it's because of the way we were.
And if now our days appear harder
it's because of the way we fare.

Jessie Morton

A Word To The Wise

One shot is all he's waiting for
The sniper on the roof
There is no hiding for the man
Whose vest is bullet-proof

A bomb primed to go off at nine
The warning's been received
Now scramble to diffuse it
No-one wants to be bereaved

All marches are contested
Over cocktails sipped at length
What you'd like to view as weakness
We would view it as our strength

All this was in the bad old days
The North of Ireland's past
We have the chance for peace
It's fragile, but it's come at last.

Kim Montia

BRISTOL BLITZ 1940

I can still see their anxious faces staring at me,
A young child brought in haste from a pre-Christmas bed.
They sat in a small tight circle; friends and ancient relatives.
Their slippered feet rested on an old threadbare carpet,
In the middle of our large damp cellar.

My grandmother, deathly still, sat upright in her velvet chair,
Now relegated like us in this desperate hour.
Their pale faces, ashened by bombers' dust, shone in the candlelight.

'Have they gone?' yelled my terrified mother,
Ears blocked by trembling fingers against the
Onslaught of the screaming bombs.
'No' someone replied; shouting to make her hear.
'Is it ours?' another wild cry went up; meaning the planes.

Patsy, my special friend, fingered her rosary,
Whilst I, copying, clutched a tin St Christopher,
Praying that God would make them go away.

A futile, but universal prayer throughout our city,
On that cold November night.

Margaret Carl Hibbs

BYGONE DAYS

The quiet roads, the leafy lanes, where we could hear the bees,
The birdsong greeting every morn from tall and stately trees.

These memories fill my heart with joy as now I sit and dream
Of days of peace when Grandma made the butter from the cream.

A little farm was tucked away amongst the fields so green
Where gentle cows and skipping lambs were ever to be seen.

If we should sometimes leave the house to visit the next farm
Our door was always on the latch and nothing came to harm.

We didn't think it difficult to light the fire each day
Or fill the lamps and trim the wicks which lit us on our way.

Under the beds the chamber pot sat there in all its glory
For toilets seemed so far away when frosty nights were hoary.

We carried water from a stream that flowed just down our lane
If water butts were empty in the summer without rain.

The peace of simple life is what my memories recall
Where each one cared and lifted up the one who'd had a fall.

Too many things have happened since those calm and peaceful days
The rushing of this modern life steals time in various ways.

So much we need the caring folk and they are still around
They still hear the birds and bees and cherish every sound.

Frieda Cox

Yo-Yo Memories

Yo-yo memories come and go.
Swapping cigarette cards,
Playing marbles in the school yard,
Boasting that you had the most,
Chicken at Christmas, as a special treat,
Now it's chicken at any time of the week,
Tilly lamps lighting, Christmas Eve shopping,
From a market stall; on the last knocking,
Buying a bruised chicken fresh, off ration, cheap,
Now it's supermarket's frozen packaged meat.

Early morning cheap workman's ticket on the trolley buses.
Now, a bus never waiting for us,
Same, as it was in the past
Waiting ages for a bus to come past.
Long trolley bus; long bamboo arm poles; remember?
Arms coming off overhead wires, now remember?
Toasting forks, toasting bread in front of an open grate,
Remember, wasn't it great?
Burning coals, cracking logs,
Chimney stacks, belching smoke, pea-soup fogs.

Coal-smut in one's eye!
How awful fog blacking out the sky,
Steam trains, smoke puffing, puffing;
Not a funny game, blind man's buff,
In our street, all traffic stopping,
Now it's traffic-stopping, grid-blocking.
News, Star Standard, from street corners shouted out,
Saturday evening soccer classified £75,000 pools pay-out.
Remember? No you don't, our yo-yo memories
Our childhood, remember your memories.

B G Clarke

MEMORIES

When I was small I can recall
I was five when I started school
I'd walk to school, then home again
There was no telly - not even a phone
But we were happy with our books and toys
There was my doll's pram, yo-yo and trains that made a noise.
'Flicks' on Saturday was one of our joys
Two pennyworth of thrills as we watched boggle-eyed
The antics of Rogers, Tarzan and vampires.
There were no needless for measles, mumps or worse
But Mum was at home to be our nurse.
Doctor would call if things were bad -
Like polio (which my brother had)
He'd charge a fee of ten bob or more
Which is now fifty pence (since '74)
Fridays it was bath night in front of the blazing grate
The copper was boiling madly so we were scrubbed
                                        and in bed by eight.
These memories are now so bitter-sweet
No fridge, car, or washing machine
But there were no break-ins nor muggers to meet
No pollution or traffic jams seen.

D A Broad

THE CORN STOOKS

When I was a child Grandpa harvested by hand
Then left the corn in stooks like gold wigwams, to stand
Then as children love to, we played hide and seek
From behind and around those corn stooks we'd peep
Then when the sun and the warm winds had dried them through
Grandpa carted them away, the threshing to do.

Valerie Ovais

A Forties' Child

From bedrooms where you saw your breath,
With windows glistening with ice,
We'd scurry, shivering down the stairs,
To dress ourselves beside our fires.

'Serviceable' - that dreaded word,
When nothing fashionable was seen
And 'so as not to show the dirt',
Our macs were navy gaberdine.

We always wore them rather long -
'To grow into' they're 'bought to last'
And in the gaps where socks fell down -
Chapped legs, where soggy hems had lashed.

We almost felt afraid to learn
At school - the teachers were so harsh
And always ready with a smack
And lavatories across the yard.

Despite all this, I would go back -
If only to escape the sight
Of this unearthly orange sky,
Polluted with the constant light.

Escape the ever-present drone
From electricity and cars -
To see a sky completely dark -
A sky where you can see the stars.

To see my mother rosy-cheeked
From toasting pikelets by the fire
And cosy silence during tea
While listening to 'Children's Hour'.

Catherine Reay

TIMES PAST

The 'good old days' or were they?
Cold bedrooms, no electricity, no central heating,
Walking to school, when skies were grey,
Vegetables and fruit from the garden, good for eating.

Happy, carefree schooldays,
Love and secrets shared, in playground fun,
Discipline the good old ways
With brothers and sisters we learned to run.

The sun was always shining, or was it?
What's for dinner? Always on our minds
First day at school feeling lonely a bit
A day at the seaside, sand, shells and other finds.

The family pets brought such joy
Cats, dogs, rabbits and fish
The first kiss, for every girl or boy
Was a time to share with friends and wish.

Open fires to keep us warm,
Mum's home cooking and apple pies
Washday blues, milk from the farm
No supermarket, no car hoping for blue skies.

Learning to ride a cycle without a care
Grazed hands, knees every day
Classroom teasing and pulling hair,
The good old days not in every way.

June Witt

Lazy Days

Remember peaceful days before the war -
lazy parks of flowering grass, 'neath trees,
when sunshine's dappling dances on the breeze
with poppies, iris, dahlias round our floor?
Children in hand-smocked organdie, with bows,
and parents, elegantly gowned and calm,
shaded by wide straw hats, and panamas . . .
where now families sit in TV rows!

Country scenes still charm, but litterbugs spoil
the grass, and massive growling cars queue near
to clutter roads and pollute ears and air.
We tire of crowds and smells of engine oil.
So mothers pat their fractious babies' backs,
from holiday excursions' toilsome tracks.

Geraldine Bruce

LANCASHIRE WAKES

No one in the neighbourhood took their annual holiday abroad
One or two weeks in Blackpool were all most families could afford
in a guest house where the landlady was a real martinet
who locked the front door at eleven each night but even yet.
I remember the excitement of the station and boarding the steam train
and that we had to stay out of the guest house even in the rain.
It wasn't much of a holiday for mothers they had to prepare the food
for the whole family of six - four children in the brood.
Sometimes Father would dig into his pocket to pay for a cart
to take us and our luggage to the station for an early start
but pennies were very scarce though we saw a different gentler man
emerging as Dad relaxed. First sight of the sea was when it all began.
We played rounders on the beach with a ball that we had brought
with us from home. I'll never know why no one ever caught
pneumonia, or worse, and there was no antibiotic.
The last day of the fortnight was always unbelievably chaotic
stuffing sandy clothes in and tying the suitcases with string
to make sure they didn't fly open scattering everything
for our friends to see. Poor people have to preserve their pride
hiding the extent of true poverty. Parents tried their best to hide
the shortages from the children. We would close the door
to keep economies secret - at what cost to the poor -
mothers who bore too many children and malnutrition
sickly children developing with small education and no ambition.
Fathers who worked for a pittance for too many hours
older siblings as substitute parents with too many powers.
They wanted desperately to leave home at the first opportunity
lacking education - repeating their history with monotonous lunacy.
To doubt the worth of parents' efforts would be an insult
and, was the struggle worth it? Look and see the result!

F B Broomfield

THROUGH THE EYES OF A CHILD

Close your eyes and think a while,
About how easy life was when you were a child.
How beautiful all creation was,
And that my friend is because.
Your life wasn't tainted and soiled,
None of your dreams were ever foiled.
There wasn't any task that couldn't be done,
Every day was a round of fun.
Your face wasn't lined with worry and strife,
Ahead of you all you could see was life.
Summers lasted forever and ever,
As children you laughed and played together.
Surrounded by animals, birds and plants,
Their beauty was something to entrance.
Magical kingdoms came to life in your mind,
And all grown-ups were trusting, generous and kind.
With no need to fret and nothing to fear,
All this fades away as year passes year.
Oh to once again be carefree and wild,
To see things as innocently as a child.

David Ford

MILL TOWN (1940)

Child of the north, the harsh moor greets its kind.
You crown with manmade rocks the brooding fell,
Beside the scanty streams. I know you well;
You were by men with granite hearts designed
To serve their purpose. Where the grey streets wind
Between the mills, the bright cloth moves to sell
Its beauty, beauty aiding beauty's spell,
Far from the source. What is the twist of mind

Which tears such splendour from the matted fleece,
Yet would not hold it? Like the dwarves that line
The sword with damascene, yet wield it not;
Or string the gems, some careless throat to please,
But not their own. Such has the drab moor got
To trudge with glories they may not divine.

John Widdows

NEWSPAPERS AND TROOPS ONLY . . .

A grey and bitter winter morn,
A dimlit station, dank, forlorn,
On platform seven the unlit coaches wait,
For stumbling, shadowy figures passing through the gate.
I find an empty seat with huddled, silent men,
Thinking of home and when they'll go again.
Sleepless, they're on parade at eight,
The engine's heat and light they patiently await.

The carriage jolts, dim bulbs emit an eerie light
On dusty seats and faces drawn and white.
Two Yankee airmen slump in corner seat,
An empty whisky bottle by their feet.
A sailor sleeps across his kit bag, looking old,
The rest of us crouch khaki-clad against the cold.
The usual ticket inspector makes his round,
With speech defect, the butt of mocking imitations
                                              of his sound.

At murky dawn, the train pulls out with our unwilling crew,
Newspapers and troops only on the 4am from Waterloo.

Peter Hicks

The Way We Were

We were happy at school until the war came,
Some lost their dads which was a shame.
A shortage of food, but worst of all
sweets were rationed amounts very small.
Mums did their best, to make things fair
when Dad had no cigs, he went up in the air.
As evacuees the schools had us go
when the day came, we went with the flow.
We were soon on our way the excitement came,
our new home loomed but it was no game.
We soon settled in but as I was small
missing my mum and that wasn't all.
Looking back through my diary, as the years passed,
some things that happened made my friends gasp.
I remember the 'Land Army' my aunt joined in,
planting and digging kept them slim.
The queues were so long for foods from afar,
we couldn't buy much packed in a jar.
As the war time ended and our men came home,
we could rejoice and smile again.
But some were still 'alone'.

Jean Calver

TOUCH THE PAST

Together we walked through the village.
'It's all different' I explained, 'This . . .
This was our factory - it was sold. Up there . . .
Up there was your grandpa's office.
He came to the window when, as a child, cycling,
I went by and shouted 'Papa' . . .

At midday the church bells always ring;
To remind the villagers it's time to eat; listen!
At midday the family always met. In the dining room
Your grandma served the meal.
She had spent all morning . . . cooking it!

After school she sent me shopping. There . . .
There's Mrs Portman's shop - all changed.
It had . . . a bit of everything!
You could pay at the end of the week
'I'll have this bar of chocolate please . . .
Could you write it down . . .' and Mrs Portman did.
Across the road is the village dairy.
Still the same. Same few steps you've got to climb.

The door has changed. I queued for fresh milk
At the end of each day -
Holding a milk can . . . talking to friends . . .
Watching the farmer's dog pull the cart
Overloaded with churns - daily routine.

Further on the right, the bakery. Amazingly
Not altered. Same name. Only -
Different generation. 'Chez Steiner' . . .
What they had was nice! In the evening at eight,
The church bells always rang. Telling us children
It was time to go in. We didn't argue.

Claire-Lyse Sylvester

WHERE?

Where has the love and friendship gone
That we used to have?
Where are all the helping hands gone,
But oh so sad.

We used to 'help each other
In any way we could.
But, now we're all too busy
And it's quite understood.

Our neighbours aren't so friendly,
As they used to be
I don't know what has happened
It's not the same for you, and me.

Now we pass a person by
And we don't give a damn
Why is this, I don't know
We should help them,
               if we can.

E B Holcombe

I Remember

Do you recall days gone by
When we were in our teens?
High-heeled shoes and make-up,
And the tightest style in jeans?
And do you remember when we both,
Danced the night away?
Ballroom dancing it was out,
Rock and Roll was here to stay.

Remember when we dressed up,
In the fanciest of clothes?
Frilly skirts and undies,
And the latest style in hose?
And how we went out dancing,
On a double date?
Making any kind of excuse,
So we could stay out late?

What about when we were kids,
And joined the Sunday School.
So we could go on the picnic?
Back then we were no fools.
What about our neighbourhood,
And the pranks we used to play?
Those things we used to do
I remember to this day.

M Muirhead

Saturday Morning

Pyramid, Palace, Warwick, Savoy
Paradise there for Saturday joy
Hopalong Cassidy, Buck Rogers with Indians to seek
Flash Gordon and Ming and wait till next week.
An occasional organ would rise from the pit
See the Three Stooges for knockabout wit.
Abbott and Costello you must imitate
The Marx Brothers especially great.
Pathé Pictorial or Movietone News
Extolled the war in black and white views.
Ollie and Stan and a sad little tramp
It was warm inside out of the damp.

Pyramid, Palace, Warwick, Savoy
Lowered lights and girl could meet boy
Saturday mornings without mums and dads
Whistle and stamp, indulge your fads.
Trigger and Lassie, Silver and Tonto
'Hi partner' and 'See you pronto'
Cinemas gone from the township of Sale
Now only TV where home comforts prevail.

Temperance billiards with the Lido to swim
Trollies and trams but the sirens were grim
Bringing aerial dogfights, shrapnel and parachute mines
Coupons for sweets and grocery lines
Few ounces of meat but back to the tramp
Queue up for Saturday morning, whistle and stamp
Popeye, Pluto, that Blackfriars scamp
Radio plays, cricket or football to pass afternoons
ITMA for fun or Disney cartoons, that war was no joy
Showing at the Pyramid, Palace, Warwick and the Savoy.

John Aldred

WHISPERING MEMORIES

The time is nineteen twenty two .. .
No tele and no radio.
Cars - solid tyres, no synchromesh!
Class fixed by birth; seldom changed

The Church too shared the class divide.
Most top people were Anglicans
Methodists had most impact
but were divided - Wesleyan
and Primitive: they seldom mixed

Change was slow; The Nation stirred when
Men - blind, without arms and legs and
worse! were seen begging on the streets . . .
A determined resolve was born.

The voice of the Nation rose clear.
The Unions formed a party
Fought hard for recognition, and
gained much support from all sections

A big help in future change
was the coming of Radio
joined quite soon by television.
The somewhat rusticated man
was soon one of greater vision.

The second World War - vile, evil . . .
Rationing, bombing, much heartache
And enormous National loss . . .
The longed-for victory - at last.

From the Tolpuddle Martyrs to
the coming of the Common Man
so many changes! But do we
want an equal society?

Collin West

ORANGES

I hadn't seen an orange
When I was small
During the war
You couldn't find them all.

After it was over
I saw one in a shop
I fell in love
With that orange.

This love affair won't stop
I love the colour,
I love the shape,

I love the taste,
The segments fair!
The war is over
Who really won?

Rationing is over
Now for some fun.

My orange it symbolises
Freedom and life.

But remember those
Who won't taste my orange
They lie in the ground
Cold and lost . . .

Remember them always
As you buy your wares
Those, who gave their lives.

Take care of what they left you
Honour their souls
Be peaceful to others
Take up their cause.

B Neave

HOME

Home was Welsh stone: one up one down
with a bit of an outhouse at the back
where my mother cooked. It overlooked
the house behind: kind of back-to-back
lacking even basic privacy

Just my mother, my father and me
the loo was in the bare backyard -
it was greenless, apart from the weeds
growing through cracks in the paving
the winters were hard

My mother scrubbed the front step
and brass fender darned and mended
my father's pit vest and polished and washed
everything until it shone like a new pin

And with an old tin of pennies she'd buy
fresh meat and fish and I can still smell
the stewing dishes wafting from the hob

Everything was my mother's job
and before my father black with coal
opened the latch this sweet soul
carried buckets from the bosh
and brought out the old tin bath
to wash away the grime

And on Mondays I'd watch the washing
blowing on the line and I'd hear the iron
spitting on the grate; my clothes were clean -
and pressed: and food was always on my plate

Sleeping: the slashing rain rattled through the sash
but when the door shut tight on the blanket of night
my home held me safe in its keeping.

Barbara King

POLICEMEN SMILED

When I was a child,
The policemen smiled.
Traffic wardens stopped and waved,
Those were the days.

Playing in dens beneath table legs,
Hiding from ghosts under bedspreads,
Cycling up and down the lane,
Taking grazed knees to Mum again.

Blackberrying in autumn,
Sledge rides before the spring,
Playing with lambs on my uncle's farm,
Freedom before term begins.

Jesus' eyes in the old church,
That followed wherever you sat,
Sitting up straight in the sermon,
Singing in my special choir hat.

Sunday School and action songs,
Dressing up in sheets,
Christmas carol singing
Up and down our streets.

Mince pies and roast dinners,
Amazing Christmas trees,
Father Christmas' stocking,
Walks in an icy breeze.

Stories in the firelight,
That crackled in the hearth,
Secret castles, maidens, knights,
And Dad's resounding laugh.

Fiona Bower

The Picture Palaces

I'll take you to the pictures now for one last gala show
Most of them are gone now or turned into bingo
But take one last lovely look and journey back with me
To see again the silver screen and those halls that used to be

The Pavilion was the place that I saw Bella Lugosi and Co
Boris Karloff gave us a fright to the delight of those in the back row!
We went there once to see the great King Kong, me and a bunch of the boys
We weren't in there very long when we got chucked out, for making a noise

Remember the Roxy? We called it the 'Ranch' where Gene Autrey used to warble
There was Roy, Trigger and the Hopalong bunch and you didn't ask for a seat but a saddle
There was Charles Starette, Smiley Burnett, Tom Mix, Buck Jones and Johnny Mack-Brown
With their guns and guitars I'll never forget how they sang a song before the big showdown

Across the street was the Kings it cost thrupence to sit in the 'Gods'
Where Cagney kills and Jolson sings and lasses met their lads
I remember the Saturday serials - Flash Gordon versus Emperor Ming
with my little bag of mint imperials I sat there like a king

When the Regal cinema was on the go we often queued there in the rain
While buskers put on a street side show and danced and played a sweet refrain
Inside we saw Abbott and Costello, Bob Hope and Bing Crosby were great
As they strolled down the road to Morocco we laughed and rolled in our seat

But the La Scala was the place to go. The one I liked the best
Three times a week they changed their show; four times I changed my vest

It was there I saw Gone With The Wind, the Roaring Twenties with gangsters galore
Sadly this palace was the last of its kind, so eyes down for we'll see them no more.

William W M Campbell

THOSE WERE THE DAYS

I still recall when I was small ~
Against the house I bounced my ball,
And chanted 'rollsy, clapsy',
And 'round the world and backsy'.
(Mother's patience sorely tried
As 'thud, thud, thud' was heard inside!)
Then came skipping in the playground,
Long rope turning round and round.
Children jumping all together,
Shouting rhymes about the weather;
Always counting up to twenty,
Making sure the rope was 'empty'.
And, if you ever fell at play,
You would surely rue the day;
The dreaded tincture was applied
(Do you remember how you cried?)
'Twas not the cut made you call out ~
But iodine that made you shout!
Then came the war and every child,
Gas mask in hand, to shelter filed.
And, underground, shared dingy lamp
With daddy-long-legs and the damp.
That dreadful siren spoiled our games
(We called old Hitler naughty names!)
At home, all curtains closed up tight,
Showing not a chink of light.
Air-raid wardens in the streets;
Food was rationed . . . even sweets!
But folks were friendly and ~ what's more ~
You *never* had to lock your door!

Those were the days!

Anne Brown

THE WAY WE WERE
(Reflections on the 50th anniversary of the Normandy landings)

A day to remember, a day of great glory,
For the past seven days we've relived their story.
We've read it in the papers, we've seen it on TV,
Fly passes by the Spitfires and wreaths laid in the sea.
A bombardier from Bolton, a corporal from Stoke,
'We've come to see old Tommy, a really smashing bloke;
They got him as he left the landing craft at nine,
The poor unlucky bastard, he stepped right on a mine,
A lovely man, a kindly man, very, very brave,
We've bought a bunch of flowers and put them on his grave.'
The high spot was the veterans marching past the queen,
Be-ribboned chests of medals, all musing on the scene
Of glorious long ago, now part of history,
They saved the world for others, the likes of you and me.
As they marched past the dais there was purpose in their stride,
Some walking, some on crutches, but their eyes were filled with pride.
Scores and scores of veterans, returned to keep a date,
And the youngest was Arthur, a sprightly sixty-eight.

Michael Carter

War

The year was nineteen thirty nine
The world on the move lives on the line
Men were in motion, women had no notion
Will our loved ones come marching home
We were at war what had life left in store?
Out went the lawns and the flowers, in went the veg
A nation at war has to be fed
No Wendy house for me, an Anderson shelter it had to be
A stone floor with three bunk beds was my play house
I remember only happy times with plenty of laughter
As I played in that hole in the ground
Mum and Nan worked at the same place
They made asbestos gloves for men fighting fires
No talk of danger from asbestos gloves then
Danger came overhead in formation
I thought it a game learning to count
We watched them go over to London from Slough
Nan said 'Don't worry hinny it's only one of ours'
Looking back why did it have a funny sign on its side
I helped in the garden and feeding the chicks
Two ounces of butter, dried eggs and such like
How did they manage to serve up a feast
My world was of women they did all the jobs
I was five years old when I met my dad
I still remember him coming back home
Holding my hand in the other our Jan's
Looking down in surprise at two girls by his side
Out of the house popped my mum with a smile
With a catch in his throat and a tear in his eye
He simply asked her 'Which one?'

Margaret Roe

CHRISTMAS LONG AGO

When I was just a little girl, Christmas was just great,
We all believed in Santa Claus, we knew he wouldn't be late.
Mam would give a pillowcase to each of us for bed,
Then kiss us, say 'Goodnight, God bless, now rest your weary head.'
We tried to keep awake, of course, but sleep quite quickly came,
Now Christmas is still special, but it's really not the same.

It always seemed so clean and white, with just a bit of snow,
On Christmas morning we would have, that truly Christmas glow.
A scooter for my sister, and also one for me,
Made by our uncle Walter, a clever man was he.
For he worked in a foundry, and they were made of steel,
I never will forget that day, and how it made me feel.

My dad had made lead soldiers, he painted every one,
The love that went into this act, forever lingered on.

We always had some little gifts, and yes, a shiny penny,
An orange, and some hazelnuts (poor kids who hadn't any)
We had a nice selection box, which we ate far too soon,
Then all had Christmas dinner, late in the afternoon.

Christmas was very special, the winters not so so mild,
And truly we did celebrate, the birth of Christ, the child.

Eileen Burton

The Way We Were

In my village years ago
Life was peaceful, quiet and slow.
Now where car and lorry speed
We only saw the friendly steed.

A traction engine rattled by
Much steam escaping to the sky.
We'd marvel at its mighty power
Nipping along at five miles per hour.

To school and back we'd walk week day
It took about an hour each way.
We'd do our sums and learn to read
Got a whack with the cane if we didn't heed.

Lift paraffin lamps to see at night
Now flick the switch, on comes the light.
The modern mom would housework hate
To beat the rugs, blacklead the grate.

Our washing done in big old tub
On piece of board the clothes we'd rub.
The wooden dolly our clothes did tangle
Then squeeze them out on big old mangle.

The loo was down behind the hedge
On through the garden full of veg.
Now all modern, top of stair
If rain or snow we don't despair.

At weekend on the farm we'd work
Foreman saw we didn't shirk.
We'd pick the fruit or stack the hay
And run back home with sixpence pay.

In days gone by to live was harder
Sometimes with little food in larder.
But all were friends and no-one foe
Where did those lovely old times go?

Geoff Rivers

ONE DAY AT A TIME

Were they really,
the good old days,
that my mama talks about.

When 'boys were boys',
and 'girls were girls',
and you always knew the man next door.

A time when church,
on Sunday morning,
was the highlight of the week.

An era of 'open doors',
and 'open hearts'?
or maybe not.

Were the old days,
as good as they said
or just a memory faded by time?

A time when minds,
were closed to life,
outside their cosy world.

So was it really,
better back then?
We'll never know,
so enjoy what we have,
remember the past,
but live your life,
one day at a time.

Claire Marie O'Connor

SUBMISSIONS INVITED
SOMETHING FOR EVERYONE

POETRY NOW '99 - Any subject,
any style, any time.

WOMENSWORDS '99 - Strictly women,
have your say the female way!

STRONGWORDS '99 - Warning!
Age restriction, must be between 16-24,
opinionated and have strong views.
(Not for the faint-hearted)

All poems no longer than 30 lines.
Always welcome! No fee!
Cash Prizes to be won!

Mark your envelope (eg *Poetry Now*) *'99*
Send to:
Forward Press Ltd
1-2 Wainman Road, Woodston,
Peterborough, PE2 7BU

**OVER £10,000 POETRY PRIZES
TO BE WON!**

Judging will take place in October 1999